A JIGIT WITHOUT HIS HORSE

THE JIGIT

PARTRIDGE
A Penguin Random House Company

Library of Congress Control Number: 2014937440
ISBN: Hardcover   978-1-4828-9684-8
                 Softcover   978-1-4828-9644-2
                 eBook   978-1-4828-9645-9

To order additional copies of this book, contact
Toll Free 800 101 2657 (Singapore)
Toll Free 1 800 81 7340 (Malaysia)
orders.singapore@partridgepublishing.com

www.partridgepublishing.com/singapore

Contents

Preface

I have dreams, though lofty, that are yet to be realized. If ever there is any of significance, it is the completion of this precious book, ranked as my biggest feat. I have neither money nor asset to leave for my children when I am gone. As a matter of fact, I am truly a Jigit without his mount. Perhaps, that was the reason why I had to finish this book, so that I could leave something, as a gift, for my children when they look to their ancestry.

During my early childhood, I lived through what is defined as hardcore poverty, with primitive ecosystem where deprivation was the order of the day. My parents, then, with their families cleared the jungles and set up a settlement where they lived from hand to mouth. Diseases and hardships were abound. Such settlements grew in numbers to become villages and later developed into small towns. It was at the same time, in the 1960s, there was an insurgence mounted by the communist activists, instituting guerrilla warfare, and took their struggle through the jungles.

Such shocks, horror, and life threatening atmosphere were the breeding ground in my formative years.

I was privileged to go through my secondary education in town that prepared me later to read history and international relations in the University of Malaya, whose vice-chancellors, then, came from nothing less than Oxbridge. This is a real game changer for me. I suppose, it was natural for me to have a career in diplomatic and foreign service, beginning with my posting in Moscow during Gorbachev's era when Soviet Union was a socialist state. However, when I returned 16 years later, in 2003, after serving in Uzbekistan, Kazakhstan and Kyrgyz Republic, Russia was a different country. My life cycle was punctuated with abrupt changes and at each phase I could sense elements of transformation in my mind set.

Notwithstanding, it is my wish that the readers would be able to relate themselves with the stories, anecdotes and travel notes that I have recorded during 17 years of my stay in Russia and Central Asia, thereby likewise, would strive towards making our world a more enlightening place for all.

I would like to express my gratitude to my friend, Yahya Mat Hassan for his ever confidence in the value of the book, enabling me to complete it.

Kuala Lumpur, October 2013.

Chapter 1

My Childhood Days

A s a young boy, my adventurous antics had always landed me in trouble. While other boys made bamboo cannons, as a way to mark the breaking of fast during Ramadan, I deviated and developed my very own "a-bomb", with half a kilogram of carbide as the main ingredient. The carbide is reactive to water; when mixed, it produces gas-emitting chemical reaction that will explode when ignited. The "bomb" was then tested; it was a successful "project". The explosion was so powerful that the whole village experienced a minor tremor. Karma bit back that day. Sadly, the magnificent "bomb" triggered a mild heart attack to an elderly woman who lived nearby.

When Muhammad Ali knocked down George Foreman in Congo (Zaire), we organized our very own version of the boxing tournament. My self-made gloves from old towel weren't factory-perfect. I think they must have caused severe injuries to my opponent's eyes. Mat Tok Abu's black eyes were much worse than Anwar Ibrahim's.[1] What followed

---

[1]   Dato' Seri Anwar Ibrahim was Malaysia's former Deputy Prime Minister who was beaten blue and black by the Inspector General of Police while in custody.

was more than a month's worth of pain, especially to the ears. Endurance was an understatement that time, as I had to tolerate his mother's soul-wrenching curses, and rich foul vocabularies, which she gladly gave whenever I passed by his house. It was the reward for hurting her only child. However, being one of the toughest guys in our village, Mat Tok Abu never shed any tear. He was really tough and fearless; it was the reasons why I preferred him to be in my company. If a particular stunt seemed to be too dangerous of an act, like when I wasn't sure whether a branch of a tall mango tree would give way (break) during our climb, Mat Tok Abu would be given the privilege to lead first. He fell from tall trees numerous times, and suffered many injuries, but Mat Tok Abu was no quitter. I got to know later that he joined the Police Commando VAT 69 (VAT is an abbreviation of Very Able Troop; the fame combat troop which played an important role in the history of Malaysia during Communists insurgencies). However, later he was demoted to a regular cop for indiscipline. I met him recently and to my amazement, he was still a Private; the lowest rank in the Police force, despite being in service for over 30 years! The latest news that I heard of him was that he got transferred to a remote Police Station in Gua Musang[2], after severely whacked an illegal immigrant in a scuffle. It seems he hasn't changed much!

I almost killed my own father by accident during one of my adventures. It was the time when I was asked to guard his *padi huma* (a kind of dry rice cultivated on the hill slope) plantation. Other than chasing away invading monkeys and birds, there was nothing else I could do.

---

[2] Gua Musang is situated in Kelantan, one of the states in East Coast of Malaysia.

Soon, boredom hit me hard, as I was alone on the isolated hill without any friend or entertainment. Transistor radios were a luxury item back then, of which my parents could not afford. Of course, mobile phone was not invented yet. The day's worth of emitted sounds of chirping wild birds plus other jungle inhabitants became lesser than appealing to the ears.

Finally, I found a pleasant piece of fund i.e rolling down rocks from the top of the hill and listening to its crushing sound as the rocks smashed the objects below. Soon I ran out of small rocks and started to look for bigger ones.

Apparently, I discovered that bigger rocks can give better thrills, as they crashed harder and louder, and were more exciting to watch, as they travelled much slower and longer down the hill. There was this huge rock about the size of a small car that I had been trying to roll down for the past three days. It didn't budge, so I dug a hole under its base. When it began to move, I placed a large branch between the rocks and then spin the huge rock down the hill.

With all the excitements and discovered strengths, I unleashed the huge rock down the slope. Suddenly, to my horror, I saw my father's figure standing right on its track, as the huge rock made its thunderous way down. In a split second, my father avoided the rock by jumping on top of a fallen tree. Suddenly, the fast-rolling rock hit a tree trunk and changed its course. As a guided missile, the rock headed straight for my father. I saw him dived as the rock was plunging towards him. I panicked and trembled for a few seconds, while wondering about my father's fate. Suddenly, he sprung up like an injured tiger from under the fallen tree and rushed towards me while waving a *parang* (machete) in his hand.

At that time, the rock was travelling at break-neck speed down the hill. Suddenly, there was a big thud and all was quiet. The stone must have hit one of his durian trees. My father who froze in his track as he heard the loud thump soon charged forward and screamed . . .

"You animal! . . .".

I couldn't recall how I escaped from father's wrath, but I was pretty sure that by the way I raced for my life, any Jamaican sprinter would find me worthy as an opponent. It was only after midnight that I returned home, while quietly slipping into the kitchen to look for food. That night, the cow shed was my bedroom. By the way, the rock is still there; a half-buried monument in my father's durian orchard. I would have a good chuckle every time I see the rock. Perhaps father did remember the eventful day too, after surviving the incident and led a long life. Alas, he succumbed to a condition called sepsis secondary to perforated ulcers and died in May 2012 at the age of 78. It was a state when his swelling appendix burst open, and his unstable heartbeats made it impossible for the doctors to perform any surgery.

I was not the only juvenile delinquent in my village. Along with Mat Tok Abu, my two cousins Abdul Rauf and Suhaimi also belonged in the same category. You could say that birds of a feather flock together. Abdul Rauf was also part of the Field Force Commando VAT 69, but he was forced into early retirement due to a dislocated shoulder during an operation. His younger brother Suhaimi is still in the Police Force, after being demoted twice. Perhaps his past juvenile tendencies are still within him at present.

In another story in a particular day, my father's bicycle tyre went flat. Father decided to change the tube, as it was rather old and patch-ridden. I took the old rubber tube and cut it into two strips about 1.5cm wide and 30cm in length. The rubber strips were then tied to a Y –shaped branch at one end, and a placed a small piece of leather at the other. In the end, I have my very own self-made catapult, with marble-sized clays as ammos.

Now my creation was ready for testing. I ventured into the nearby woods to look for birds and squirrels. After wandering around for about an hour, the catapult remained untested. As the evening was hot, I assumed that the birds and other animals were resting in their domain. On the way home through a rubber plantation, I took a few aimless shots at anything that crossed my path. Suddenly, I saw from afar a huge hornets' nest dangling from a rubber tree. I took cover in a nearby bush and began to shoot at the nest. After a few missed shots, I managed to hit the target and made a hole through the nest. The enraged hornets scrambled out of their home to scout for the invader. I froze as the angry insects circled around and made threatening buzzes.

When the situation was calmer, I rose out of hiding and launched another strike. This time, a bigger hole was made, and prompted thousands of angry hornets to rush out to search for the culprit. I dived to the ground and played dead for awhile. When it felt safe to move, I sprinted out of the rubber plantation, and made way towards the *padi* (rice) fields.

While still out of breath, I came across a swampy area; a popular breeding ground for fighting fish. I started to look for pool of bubbles on the water surface. The reason was because in normal circumstances, that is where you can find beautiful male fighting fish guarding the eggs. So, while cupping both palms together, I gently scooped the fighting fish under the bubbles; one of many techniques to catch the fish. I took a large taro leaf, folded it, and filled it with water to keep my new pets.

When I was done and contented, I would choose only a couple of the most beautiful fully grown fish, and released the rest back into the water and ran home. Then, before I could finish transferring the last fighting fish into a glass jar, I heard a loud scream from my mother;

" Look at you . . . . dirty like a water buffalo from head to toe . . . . You better wash . . . .";

Before she could finish, I already sprang out to safety, and ran towards a well that was about 100 meters away. The last thing that I saw was my mother's stout figure bending down to pick up a branch. Experience has made me wiser; I knew that the branch would end up on my back, and I should also wait at a safe distance, and proceed to hear her sermons from afar.

Apparently, the episode with the hornets' nest did not end there. The next morning, a few unlucky rubber tappers entered the area, and encountered the wrath of the furious insects. One of them has the reputation of being the most hot-tempered man in my village. The first thing that I did was to hide the catapult and pretended to be dumb. Although many suspected that I was the culprit, they didn't have any proof, as nobody saw me in action. An old woman, a distant relative of mine, asked what I was doing the day before. I calmly answered that I spent the whole evening catching fighting fish in the swamp after school, followed by the cat and mouse chase between my stick-equipped mother and me. Someone supported my story, and told her that she saw me washing dirty clothes at the "public bath" (a place with one of the two public wells in the village) on the said evening. It was a silver lining in disguise, as even though in the 60's, most of Malaysian villages did not have piped water or electricity, luckily enough, the situation endowed me with a good alibi . . . .

Later that day, a good Samaritan took a long bamboo pole, tied dried coconut leaf at the tip, lit it on fire, and burned down the hornets' nest. The act was necessary, as without it, many would be scared to work at the rubber plantation. When the nest was brought down, some women collected the larvae from the hornets' nest as bait for fishing. I quietly thought that it was not a bad thing after all.

Our mischief became the topic of discussion among the elders. But somehow, I was the target for most of the blames; much to the disappointment of my mother. One day, a few boys plundered a sugar cane plantation of one of the villagers. As expected, I was the main suspect. My mother was so upset that she made a remark, saying that none of her family members were known to be thieves. I was also hurt by the allegations. My mother then advised me to study hard and move away from the rural life.

Life felt ironic, especially when I was enrolled at a primary school named "Sekolah Kebangsaan Kepala Batu" (Kepala Batu National Primary School), named after the village where the school was located in a rural District of Kubang Pasu, Kedah[3]. Kepala Batu means "Stone Head". It is also a Malay proverb. We were endlessly ridiculed and teased during inter-school events, such as sport competitions and stuffs. When we marched at Darulaman Stadium during the Annual Sports Competition, students from other schools would tease us as our contingent passed by them . . . .

---

[3]   Kedah is located in the North Western part of Peninsular Malaysia.

"Sekolah Kebangsaan Kepala Batu, meaning those stubborn fellas . . . ."

As anticipated, sometimes it ended with brawls. If I am not mistaken, in the 1980's, the education authorities decided to rename the school with a more appropriate name for an education establishment. Now it is named Sekolah Kebangsaan Sri Banai. Nevertheless, I was proud to be the first student from the "Stone Head" Primary School who succeeded in entering the oldest and most prestigious university in the country at that time. My younger brothers who followed suit later on told that my name was engraved on the wall in one of the old blocks. I guessed it is no longer there now, as the old wooden blocks were demolished in order to build a bigger school.

Despite the fact that I was not that diligent in my studies, I was fortunate enough to gain admission to the University of Malaya, Kuala Lumpur. It was very tough in those days to enter a university. I remembered a teacher, our hostel master (warden) who had to sit for HSC (High School Certificate) Examination for eight consecutive years, before he was finally qualified to enrol at a local university. Our hostel warden, M Mydeen was so proud and overjoyed when I met him at Puduraya Bus Station[4] in late 70's, as he has just arrived from Alor Star to start his courses.

During a semester break, I returned to the village with a new perspective in life. Nonetheless, I still remember a remark made by an aunt who had always empathised with

---

[4]   The Puduraya bus terminal (now renamed to Pudu Sentral), located in the city centre and used to be KL's main bus station. After a complete make-over and the re-opening in April 2011, it now servers north-bound buses.

me when I was hurled with various accusations by the kampung folks. [5] She said;

"Last time, they (the village's elders) used to blame you for all the mischief in the village. Now, even though you are not around, unbecoming incidents are still happening. Three days ago, some boys slaughtered my chicken and had a barbeque in the rubber plantation. The boys didn't put off the fire completely, and the whole rubber plantation would have been destroyed by the fire if not for Pak Hamid who happened to pass by the place . . .

I just smiled, but not without a sense of remorse for all of my childhood pranks in the past. I was happy to leave my childhood and the village life in searching for a meaningful life in the city.

Once, during one of the holidays, I visited "Ah Chun", a Chinese trader in Jitra, who used to buy our rice and rubber. I greatly admired this man for his kindness in helping the Malay farmers during the challenging times. Tauke[6] Ah Chun had established a close bond with the Malay farmers around the district who became his customers. He never missed any invitation to attend all of the wedding dinners in the villages. He was not the type of middlemen who would exploit poor farmers, especially those who constantly lived and faced uncertain economic hardships.

The Tauke's remarks is still ringing in my ears. He said that he was proud to see me enter the university. He also told me that if I ever needed financial help, I could come to him directly, without having to burden my father with the problem. He said that he had great respect for my

---

[5]   villagers

[6]   Tauke is referring to a merchant or trader and it is commonly
       used for Chinese trader in Malaysia.

father; a person known to be hardworking and trustworthy. However, Tauke Ah Chun had a small favour to ask of me. He made me promise that I would cut my hair short after completing my university education. He said, since I would be an important person, I must look neat and smart. He added that if it's possible, he suggested that I return to my hometown to become a District Officer and serve the community.

It was a "hippy" era during my university days. The trend showed when a lot of people spotted long hair; mine was among the longest in the campus.

"I will never be a pillion rider with you again. Your long flowing hair was splattering all over my face that I could hardly breathe!", said an uncle who once hitched a ride on my bike.

During those days, it was not mandatory to put a crash helmet when riding a motorbike.

Unfortunately, Tauke Ah Chun did not stay long enough to see me fulfil his wish. One day, Tauke Ah Chun had to quietly sneak out of the town in the middle of the night with his whole family members, when he discovered that one of his sons busted the family business. He simply could not face the community, after losing his "honour". Till today, his whereabouts is never known. My father had always reminded us to settle his outstanding debts amounting to about RM200, should one day we manage to meet the runaway Tauke.

Chapter 2

The First Job

My first job was at the Petaling Jaya Municipality (MPPJ), now elevated to City Council. I was given general duties including those of Administration and Enforcement. There was a box, placed in my room that became the subject of squabbles among senior officers. It seemed that a few Heads of Department would like to keep the box in their rooms. In one of the meetings, I told them that they could have it if they wanted to. However, MPPJ Chairman insisted that the TENDER BOX should remain in my room. It was only later that I learnt about the significance of the box; tenders for various development projects worth hundreds of millions of ringgit were kept in the box before they were awarded to the developers. No wonder local businessmen and contractors were so friendly to me.

Although I worked at MPPJ only just for a year, but I had a few memorable experiences such as having to cremate a criminal shot by the police. As I was preparing to go out during a weekend, Majid (not the real name), the Chief Clerk came to my house and took me to a Crematorium in Section 16, Petaling Jaya. Grumbling all the way, Majid told me that the family of the dead man didn't want to claim the body and we ended up doing the dirty job. My persuasion to him that God would reward us for our good deeds failed to amuse him. The hospital staff who brought the body from the morgue helped us to put the corpse in the (oven) pit and left Majid and me to handle it from there. Still cursing, Majid switched on the fire while I was reading the newspapers.

After an hour, Majid lost his patience and prematurely opened the fire pit only to find a heap of bones instead of dust. He took a wooden plank and began to break the bones into small pieces. I hinted that it was not nice to treat the dead body that way but Majid quipped that he was only doing a favour for the Angels, doing half of the beatings on their behalf. Apparently, Majid was annoyed because the impromptu duty which fell under 'OTHER DUTIES AS INSTRUCTED BY THE SUPERIOR OFFICERS' had delayed his plan to attend a wedding ceremony. My presence there was needed to witness and certify that the job was done, unprofessionally of course!

A handsome gentleman from Taiping, Majid in his younger days was a small time playboy in Petaling Jaya. He lived at MPPJ Quarters in Jalan Gasing. One day, I bumped into him and his wife for the first time at Asia Jaya Supermarket as he formally introduced his wife to me. Having learnt about his flamboyant background, I was trying to pull a practical joke on them.

"So this is the real one I hope . . . . the last time you introduced your wife to me, she happened to be a blonde, slim and tall woman. But this one is definitely much nicer", said I as I bowed to his wife and casually walked away.

I thought the joke ended there, but apparently it didn't. The next morning Majid came to the office with red blotchy eyes and screamed at me.

"You rascal, why did you have to joke like that to my wife? She truly believes in your lies and nagged me the whole night that I could hardly sleep !".

I called up his wife to explain that the whole thing was just a joke, and I've never seen Majid with any other woman before. She replied, "You men are all the same. You would lie to protect each other, now it is too late to deny it!"

Being flamboyant, Majid took really good care of his Ford station wagon. He polished the car so regularly that his envied wife remarked one day;

"How lucky I would be if he treats me the way he looks after his car!"

There was yet another interesting character who worked at MPPJ at that time. This guy was a real genius when it came to generating side incomes. He used to drive MPPJ's steamroller to build private roads during holidays and weekends. So we transferred him to the Nursery Department. But soon he began to sell the seeds and plants under the counter. After a lengthy deliberation, we decided to send him to the Cemetery Division. Everyone anticipated that he would meet his dead end. To our amazement, he opened a shop selling tombstones. Anyway, we didn't bother him any longer as his new trade did not directly involve the abuse of power or misuse of government's property. If this man is made the Minister of Entrepreneurship, I'm sure he could do wonders!

During my time at MPPJ, there was a young botanist, if I'm not mistaken hailed from Sabak Bernam[7], Sumadi his name. Despite the fact that he was a graduate from one of

---

7   Sabak Bernam is a District of Selangor State, dominated by Javanese immigrants.

the universities in the UK, Majid and I could not help but to laugh at his thick Javanese accent when he speaks English. Later, I learnt that Sumadi left MPPJ to join corporate sector. However, there was another guy, Amir, an engineer, who was very loyal to the organization (MPPJ). I used to read in newspapers about his numerous "inventions". They called him MacGyver, named after the famous TV series character in the 80's.

"I'm number One in PJ!" claimed the MPPJ Chairman. However, the District Officer was not amused. They were engaged in a bitter rivalry over the issue of seniority in the district. Sometimes the tussles between the two Super Scale "F" PTD officers became so obvious that one would refuse to attend official events if the other party was there. When the District Office (DO) hosted a meeting, my boss, MPPJ Chairman would send me, the most junior officer to represent him, simply to snub the DO. This act would not go unretaliated.

I have a great admiration for a few dedicated Councillors. One of them was Haji Abdullah Sanggura who whole-heartedly devoted his time to serve the communities. He strenuously fought against any form of favouritism and cronyism in awarding government contracts, thereby creating "enemies" along the way. As anticipated, his service was not renewed by the Selangor State Chief Minister. This could possibly be due to a few politicians with vested-interest who were not happy with him even though he topped the list of those recommended by the Chairman for renewal of contract.

During his younger days, Haji Abdullah Sanggura was jailed in Singapore under the notorious Internal Security Acts (ISA). He was one of the earliest freedom fighters who took a hard-line approach together with Ahmad

Boestamam, Mustaffa Hussein, Burhanuddin Helmi, Ishak Haji Muhammad and many others during the struggles for our independence. Sadly, true to the tradition of a freedom fighter, Haji Abdullah Sanggura died a poor man.

I left MPPJ in December 1981 to join the Administrative and Diplomatic Service (PTD).

Chapter 3

Dobry Pozhalavat: Welcome to Moscow!

I didn't know a single word in Russian when I arrived in Moscow in early 1986. When I arrived, Gorbachev was just about to initiate reforms in the Soviet Union. The sound of Russian and Communism used to scare many people. Indeed, it was.

As I took my first step on the Soviet soil, I slipped but managed to avoid a fall on the frozen tarmac. The aircraft was parked about 400 meters from the parking bay and we had to get into the bus to be ferried into the terminal building under the watchful eyes of Soviet Border Guards.

Sherimentyevo International Airport was so gloomy that it seemed it was designed to create a mystique ambience. It sent shivers to my spine as the stern-faced woman Border Guard officer who stared at me, observing from head to toe, as she struggled to "peel" the cover of my passport in her attempt to check if it was tempered. I posed one of the sweetest smiles but the female Russian bear wasn't moved at all. After about 10 minutes of conducting thorough examination of my travel document as if she wasn't happy with the visa issued by the Soviet Embassy in Kuala Lumpur, she finally signalled to me to wait at a corner while she took my passport into a room. A few other officers with Kalashnikov rifles in their grips were watching my every move as if I was a prisoner being escorted to Siberia. After some time, I was relieved to see a familiar face of a Malaysian Embassy officer who came to meet me on my arrival.

"Don't change money in the bank. Tell me if you need Roubles". That was the first useful advice from the Embassy officer who met me when we headed for the hotel.

When the plane made a stop in the middle of the airfield and the door was opened, a few soldiers in green overcoat armed with Kalashnikov assault rifles entered and took some documents from the Pilot. They looked stern and very intimidating, as they screened every passenger as if we were the enemy of the Soviet Union. Later on I learnt that this was the manifestation of the philosophy that the State was supreme. Those soldiers were from the regiment of Border Guard Services, answerable directly to the "Komitet Gosudarstvennie Bezzoposnost[8]" or the KGB. After about 15 minutes the passengers were allowed to get off the plane under the watchful eyes of the soldiers and were directed into the waiting bus. After we were packed like canned fish in the bus, two soldiers jumped into the front seats and sat next to the driver. We were taken to the Terminal building. As we arrived, a dozen more soldiers were waiting for us.

I confided to myself;

"Is this the first layer of the Iron Curtain!"

A stout lady in blue uniform (she must be AEROFLOT ground staff) ordered us to climb a stair case hurling our hand luggage. I took pity on some passengers with children

---

[8] KGB is the Committee for the State Security.

in their arms struggling with heavy winter clothes and hand luggage. We walked in circle through a few doors before we were led to another stair case and this time we had to walk down the ground floor. Suddenly, I found that we had arrived next to the point where we started, except that we were now standing on the inside of the glass door of the terminal building. I was annoyed and wanted to demand an explanation about the rationale why from the ground floor we were asked to climb up to the upper floor, made a few detours and then came back to where we started. However, while I was weighing my courage to ask the fat lady in the blue uniform, I saw a soldier from outside approaching the locked door, took out a bunch of keys and opened it. There was some exchange of angry words between the stout lady and the soldier with the keys. In a democratic country the ground staff would have suggested that we should wait for someone to bring the key!

Again I reminded myself,

"Relax . . . . Perhaps this is the second layer of the Iron Curtain".

The journey from Syerementyevo International Airport to the city took about 45 minutes those days. Today you would be lucky if you could make it within one and the half hours. About 10 km from Syerementyevo Airport, I saw an interesting object of a large barricade made of huge iron slabs near the highway. The Embassy official who met me explained that those barricades were erected as a monument to mark the line where the German invading troops were halted in a fierce battle during the World War II. The Germans never reached the city as they were stopped at the outskirt of Moscow. The Officer added that even Napoleon army was defeated not far from that place during the famous battle of Borodino. The country has been invaded by many foreign forces, the Tatars, the Finns, the French and the Germans, but the brave and determined Russian people have never been defeated!

The roads were wide, specifically built that way to enable at least three tanks or armoured personal carriers to pass freely during war or crisis situations.

"The lamp post is so huge", I remarked to my new friend from the Embassy. He laughed and replied that the single lamp post made of solid steel like that could be used to make a few pieces in other countries. He also told me that a few years back, Japan used to import large amount of sledge hammers and lamp posts from Soviet Union. At first the Russians were proud that even the Japanese appreciated their products. However, soon they stop selling those items when they discovered that apparently, the Japanese have sent the sledge hammers and lamp posts direct to the smelters where those crude and ugly products were turn into different types of high grade steel merchandise.

I noticed there were some small houses scattered in the distance along the road. Later I learnt that they were called *dacha*, country house or summer homes belonging to the privileged and the ruling elites that served as their retreat during summer. As we approached the city line, tall residential buildings of identical designs begun to emerge. They looked dull and dreadful. One of these flats could be my home for the next couple of years, I said to myself.

There was a peculiar view in Soviet Republics where the presence of policemen was felt everywhere. Clad in thick sheepskin coats, they stood at every traffic light and every corner of the street, holding white and black stripe baton. These Traffic Police were very powerful. When they flagged down motorists, none would speed off because if they did, they would be stopped at the next junction.

It was in the middle of winter when I first arrived. There were piles of frozen ice covered with snow along the road side. For the first time I witnessed how the workers cleaned the road. Four or five trucks fixed with bucket were driven in a sliding vertical line shoving the snow from road surface, followed by another truck which sprinkled sand added with salt. Instead of using chemicals like in other European countries, the Russians were using salt to melt the frozen roads as it was cheaper. I looked at the naked branches of leafless trees lining the streets. It was a pitiful sight as if all the trees were dying. Other than some species of pines such as firs and (Christmas) tree, other plants shed their leaves during winter.

Judging from the swelling crowd at Metro (subway) stations we passed by, one could figure out that Moscow was a big city. At that time Moscow was inhibited by 12 million people plus 2 or 3 million visitors from other cities. Stern looking men and women in heavy coats were conducting their own affairs.

"Those big mamas are called *babushka* and the young girls are called *debushka*, explained my Embassy friend. I found most of the Russian people were unfriendly and rough. That was my first impression. Only later I realised that the system and surrounding environment would have moulded similar society irrespective of race or skin colour. I also noticed that Russian people loved reading. They read at every opportunity, while waiting for the bus, in Metro, some even while taking a stroll in the park.

My new friend from the Embassy was talking incessantly while I absent-mindedly listened as my brain was too busy digesting and processing the images I discerned seen along the journey. Occasionally, he would speak Russian with the driver, perhaps trying to show off his linguistic prowess.

Nevertheless I quietly admired and envied his talent to be able to speak one of the world's "exotic" languages. From that day, I was determined to learn the language.

After slightly over an hour's drive, we finally arrived at our destination, a 13-storey flat located at Obrucheva Street, not far from the Patrice Lumumba University (Patrice Lumumba became the first Prime Minister of Congo after the Republic won the independent from Belgium in June 1960. He was assassinated by firing squad four months later and the Soviet regime built a university in his honour in Moscow). During the Soviet era, the University only catered for foreign students, mostly from the African continent.

The flat looked similar to the surrounding residential blocks. However, I was told that it was a special block built for diplomats and other expatriates. My colleague told me, most of the ordinary Soviets people live in a one room flat which served as a living, as well as bedroom. The slightly privileged citizens such as the local Communist Party Chairman, Head of governmental bodies or bosses of Soviet enterprises, Chairman of Collective Farms may be given two or three-room flats. My home was a three room flat, located on the 8ᵗʰ floor facing the main road and a small pond.

I noticed, our apartment block was the only building in the area that surrounded by a three-metre fence. There was a guard house stationed at the entrance leading to the parking area. Two Policemen stood up and peeked into the car I was travelling, as they wrote something in their sketch book. Later, I learnt that diplomats and other expatriates residing in Moscow were exclusively allocated to live in the special residential blocks where their movement could be easily monitored. Russians were not allowed to enter these premises. They would be arrested and interrogated by the KGB if they did. All apartments that were allocated to the diplomats and expatriates, as well at all foreign embassy buildings were guarded by the Special Police Squad, which reported directly to the KGB. These Policemen were required to record every movement of the expatriates at their respective place such as what time so and so left his or her apartment, with whom he or she left, the model, colour and registration number of the vehicle so on so forth.

Apparently, these policemen have an album, where the photograph and the data of every occupant of that building, including the children were kept. That's why you were required to provide at least 4 copies of photograph when you applied for visa to enter the Soviet Union.

As I have lowered my expectation before coming to this country, I wasn't upset to see the sorry state of my apartment block. I guessed the flat was built shortly at the end of the World War II. I was told that, the similar flat was occupied by my predecessors way back since Malaysia established its diplomatic relations with the USSR in April 1967. However, I was slightly nervous when the old elevator gave a rude jerk when it reached on the eight floor, where my flat was located.

"Don't worry . . . it is Soviet made, the cable must be very solid and strong", remarked the colleague from the Embassy, having noticed the anxious look on my face.

I inspected all the three rooms, toilet and shower, the kitchen and quietly tried to comfort myself that everything would be fine. I soon adjusted to the new environment with ease and begun to enjoy new adventures.

Chapter 4

Outing in the Country Side

Those days, foreigners residing in Moscow were only allowed to travel within 40 km radius of Outer Ring Road. If one needs to travel outside this perimeter, an Official Note must be dispatched to the Foreign Ministry citing reason for the journey, members of travelling party, vehicle registration number, precise date and routes to be taken. For holiday in the country side, a special resort in Zavidovo situated about 200 km from Moscow has been built specifically to cater for the expatriates.

The Malaysian community in Moscow used to book a few chalets in Zavidovo during winter, learning to ski and in summer, going for fishing or collecting mushroom in the woods.

There were about twenty Traffic Police check points along the 200 km road to Zavidovo. It was a mandatory for the Police at every post to note down the plate numbers of our vehicles including the identity of passengers. Sometimes, we were stopped and reprimanded for speeding. Once I challenged him on how he knew for certain that we were speeding. But then I realized, his colleague at the previous post must have alerted him when we just passed. So if we reached the following check point earlier than the estimated time, obviously we have exceeded the speed limit. And if we did not arrive at the check point within stipulated time, a car would be sent to track us down. The rule was clear that we were not supposed to stray from our itinerary. We were not supposed to stop for a short rest at the road side, fearing that we might have a clandestine meeting with the agents or trying to sabotage some strategic installations in the country site. I guessed the Russians must have certain installation in place in some parts of the road. It was a rigid rule but on the other hand, it was good for us because if our car broke down or having a flat tire in the mid of winter, without having to make a frantic phone call, the help would arrive in five minutes.

We had a lot of fun for having "Abang Baha[9]", husband of the Embassy's Chief Clerk with us. One day we decided to try mushroom gathering in the woods. Normally people would go in pairs or in groups for this activity. As the woods covered quite a large expanse, one could get separated easily from one's friends and therefore they keep shouting or calling out each other's name. This friendly "Abang Baha" had been responding to a guy's shout for about an hour or so until the guy finally showed up in front of him.

"Oh shit! Were you the one who has been responding to my call all this while?" he asked.

Failing to understand what the Russian man said, Abang Baha shouted for my rescue. First, he thought that the man's approach was just a friendly act. However, when the man started to scream and curse, only then he realized something must have gone wrong. Apparently, the man was mad at Abang Baha for responding to his shouts as

---

9   Abang means older brother in Malay.

he discovered that he had "lost" his friend in the woods. I calmed him down by telling him that it was our first venture in mushroom gathering and we simply thought that shouting was part of the fun.

After about two hours, we came out from the woods and approached a few local men who took a break near the river bank. Abang Baha showed a basketful of colourful mushrooms he collected and suddenly the Russians broke into laughter. They told us those colourful mushrooms were poisonous. One of them began to throw away the inedible mushrooms from the basket. In the end, he held up the only one bud left, the ugliest looking one and told us that it was a good one. They again burst into laughter when I informed them that we had spent about two hours in the woods only to take home one piece of mushroom. The Russians showed us edible mushrooms which we had mistakenly thought to be rotten.

Again the situation became comical when Abang Baha suddenly took out from his pocket a handful of baby frogs collected from the woods. The men became hysterical when one of them remarked that now these "Vietnamese" were going to fry the frogs instead of mushrooms. When I explained that the baby frogs would be used as baits for fishing, the Russians again laughed at us. He said they never used frogs as baits.

We really had fun while taking our first lesson to ski. Just imagined those funny tumbles and awkward falls. I quit after accidentally breaking one of the skiis. It could have been my legs, next . . .

Another thrilling experience was having sauna during winter. First, we sit in a real hot sauna room and endured the "pain" until we could no longer stand the heat. At this moment, we would rush out of the bath house and dive into piles of snow, making "hissing" sound. After the "cooling off" period, we returned to the sauna room. Again, when the heat was unbearable, we rushed out but this time we took a dip in icy water of Moscow River. Oh boy, I really missed the fun!

Sometimes, the Soviet Foreign Ministry would organize a special hunting trip at the resort for Diplomats. The Russians would release a few tame animals such as deers probably from a nearby collective farm or wild boars from the zoo into the woods, as the game animals hardly ran away upon meeting the noisy huntsmen. Once I joined the hunting trip but stopped the practice the following year when a Diplomat was shot in the leg by one of the amateur colleagues.

Chapter 5

My Tatar Friend

As I entered one of the oldest mosques in Russia, located next to the Moscow Olympic Stadium at Mir Avenue, my eyes closely examined the interior decoration of the building, before shifting my view and observe other members of the congregation. A majority of them were strikingly grey-haired old men of Tatar descent. It was quite an experience to witness the characters of these people. It was a normal sight to witness 70 year-old men fighting over petty matters in the mosque, such as taking someone's spot in the mosque, or blocking someone's view. Sometimes the quarrels gradually developed into the acts of pushing and shoving. We often witnessed the Imam's sermon being disrupted by some unhappy congregation. Apparently, the Imam had left out the old men's names when the former was reading the donors' list for that week!

On that day, I was determined to find someone who could solve one of our pressing problems. There was one man in particular that grabbed my attention the first time I laid my eyes on him. His red beard, shining red face, green eyes, plus the charismatic look, triggered my curiosity. After the Friday prayer, I immediately looked for him. I slowly approached the man, gave a greeting, and introduced myself. I can sense that his alert eyes were scouting around like falcons. Before I could make my intentions clear, he whispered to me to mingle around for a while, and then to proceed to the ablution room in the mosque compound.

I was excited and felt like an operative secret agent in action. There were a few people inside the ablution room when I entered. Like a trained spy, I ignored the old man, but settled next to him, and pretended to perform the ablution. When other people left the room, I quickly introduced my name, and told him that we needed *halal*[10] meat supply; something that was not available at that time. His name is Abdul Haq, and from that day, he became one of my closest friends. Our relationship lasted for over 25 years, and was forged based on my deepest respect and admiration for the old man whom only a few would understand.

Abdul Haq is a devout Muslim in the land where religious worshiping was suppressed for over 70 years under Communism. He was hailed from a family with strong Muslim traditions, and was testified through the story of his late father, Idris. Abdul Haq's father had fought alongside the Red Army during the World War II against invading Germans in one of the bloodiest battles at Stalingrad (Volgograd). Once, the Communist Commanding Officer of his regiment reprimanded Idris for taking intervals to perform the solat (prayers) during a heavy battle. Idris reacted fiercely by telling the Commander that he would put the bullet in the latter's head first, before he charged

---

[10] *Halal* is an Arabic word wish means 'permissable or lawful' in Islam. In this respect, the animal was slaughtered according to the Muslim rites.

at the Fascists, should he ever again try to stop him from performing the prayers. Finally his Commander just walked away and never raised the issue again. After all, the Tatars had fought bravely during the Great War.

In order to get the supply of *halal* meat, we had to travel to "Tiche Rinok"; a crowded bazaar in Moscow suburb that sells live chicken, dogs, cats, birds and other pets. Sometimes we could find little lambs too. When we bought a few small 3-month old lambs, the Russian *babushka* (grandmother) would stop us before we could reach our cars. They began to query on what we were going to do with the cute little lambs. An experienced staff would tell the women that he wanted to keep the little lambs as pets. Once, a newly-posted Embassy Staff was too honest to gesture that he would slaughter the lamb for meals. Hell broke loose, as a few *babushkas* surrounded and hurled curses at him. Someone tried to hit that poor fellow with her handbag. I had to drag the deeply-stunned guy away from the angry crowd, while having a good laugh because of his naivety.

We slaughtered chicken, rabbit and other "pets" behind the Embassy compound, and cleaned them ourselves. It was such a hectic and messy affair over the weekends, or that was then, before I met Abdul Haq.

Once a month, we would pool our resources, and ordered a cow from Abdul Haq, who later slaughtered the animal, skinned it, and sent it to my apartment. However, it was not an easy task. It was just like a covert operation. Local people who established contacts with foreigners, especially those from the Embassy, would end up at KGB's interrogation rooms. We were careful not to get our valuable contact in trouble. On Friday, I would meet him secretly at the mosque and passed my order, as well as made arrangements on the time and place for the delivery.

As a precaution, the delivery was normally carried out late at night. Abdul Haq had to travel about 70km from his house in Domodedovo to my apartment in Leninsky Avenue. He could not enter the territory where expatriates lived. So, I had to wait for him at a predetermined meeting place.

Abdul Haq made me nervous in many occasions, when he failed to turn up, when he was a couple of hours late for a meeting. Once, I waited anxiously till 2.00 am in the middle of cold winter, and not knowing what to do next. There was no safer mode of communication. A phone call made in the middle of the night to him would only raise suspicions, as our phone calls were constantly monitored by the KGB. I almost gave up, when he suddenly turned up and covered with grease. Apparently, the old car that he rented broke down on the highway.

Abdul Haq told me that all those risky services that he did for us were not for the money, but as part of his religious duty. He never profited a single cent from us. He didn't even charge us for the long hours that he spent to prepare the meat, and delivery services. If we paid extra to him, while insisting that it was as *sedekah* (alms), he would donate the money for the construction of mosques. He said God would reward him through other channels when he helps others in need.

Our relationship with him grew deeper. When we returned to Malaysia for a break from work, we would bring back copies of Quran or religious booklets for Abdul Haq, of which he treasured with high appreciation. Sometimes during summer, I would bring a few colleagues, and we would quietly slip into the train (commuter) heading for his home in the countryside. It was really a fun moment, as we feasted on grilled lambs and other Tatar delicacies, and rode his antique Second World War Motorcycle, and finally stormed into his sauna, before returning to Moscow. We returned back home feeling exhausted, but we were happy and contented.

In 1999, after almost twelve years since I left Moscow, I made a stopover at the Russian capital from an official trip to Buryatia Republic in the Siberian region. Moscow had changed so much that I couldn't find my way to Abdul Haq's house. However, after the third attempt, I managed to stop at the right station. As I got off from the train, I saw the pathetic figure of an old man walking away from the station, with his head hung so low to the ground. While reaching for the top of my voice, I called his name. The 75 year-old man ran towards me like a small kid, with tears rolling down his face. I am a tough guy, but the reaction simply broke me down. We hugged for a very long time, while he mumbled that he came to the station twice to look for me. He complained about the pain in his legs, and his deteriorating health.

I wouldn't have found his house, if he hadn't met me at the station. His tiny little home was "hidden" among three or four-storeyed mansions built by the rich Russians, the Mafias, corrupt prosecutors, and shrewd businessmen. The little old house looked so out of place against the new castles around the area. Abdul Haq told me that he was offered good money for the land, but he refused to part with his little home. Abdul Haq narrated that there was one day, when a hen of his ventured into the neighbour's compound. He could see the bored owner who was resting on the balcony, while being half-naked and holding a bottle of vodka. As soon as the chicken entered his compound, the man laid down the bottle on the side table and rushed into his house. A minute later, he came out with a hunting rifle, and fired at the poor bird from the fourth floor of his mansion. As Abdul Haq's old woman was crying over her dead chicken, the Mafia boss who shot it came down and shoved a 100 US dollar note as compensation, without saying a word or showing any sign of remorse. The chicken could only fetch a maximum of 10 dollars each if it was still alive, but to some people, dignity was non-negotiable.

We exchanged stories and news about old friends. Before leaving, I gave 500 dollars for him to buy air tickets to visit me in Almaty, Kazakhstan where I was stationed. I promised to take care of his ailing legs. Two months later, Abdul Haq arrived and stayed at my home for three weeks. Every day I sent him for physiotherapy and massage by an Uyghur woman; the same woman who had earlier healed my twisted ankle as a result of playing rugby with the Kazakh university students. They got along well as Tatar and Uyghur languages are very close to each other.

During his stay, I went hunting and brought back 22 pheasants. While my Russian maid was still struggling to clean her first bird of its feathers, Abdul Haq had already finished his third. He returned to Moscow healthy as a bull. He revealed that he enjoyed good health for nearly two years after the treatment in Kazakhstan, before the pain in the leg returned.

The last time I met Abdul Haq was in December 2006. When we parted, he said that perhaps it would be our last reunion, as his health was deteriorating (he was already over 87 years old at that time). A couple of months ago, I made a call to a house in Domodedovo. His old woman answered my call and told me that the old man was still around despite his failing health. I couldn't speak to him, as he was visiting a relative in another town.

Only God decides who deserves His paradise. However, I used to tell friends that if they would like to see a candidate who would enter Paradise without much of a hassle, then they should have a good look at this old man, as if it is clearly written on his face.

Chapter 6

My Russian Teacher, Tamara

She was in her late forties, and a perfect model of a devoted Communist. Tamara's loyalty to the ideology was unquestionable. For that reason, she was allowed to teach Russian to foreigners. Tamara wore Soviet-made odd-looking glasses, and unfashionable locally-made suits. If I were to say something about the French fashion, she would cut it short by asserting that "Soviet-made dress is always practical and reliable, as they are made from original materials". There was no point in arguing with her, as she had totally shut off her mind from accepting anything that is foreign.

My colleagues used to ask me why I employed such an old woman as my Russian teacher. My reply was brief; I wanted to concentrate on my studies. Sticking out my tongue, I said; "Learning Rusky Yazik[11] from a young female teacher could be very distracting you know . . ."

Somehow, the "marvellous" smell of Tamara's perfume *Krasnaya Moskva* (Red Moscow) mixed with summer sweats often caused me to lose my concentration. In order

---

11   Rusian language which also means Russian 'tongue'

to counter the smell, I sprayed a lot of French perfume on my suit, every time I had a class with Tamara. Perhaps she took it as an inviting challenge between French and Soviet products that she increased the volume of her perfume, forcing me to open all of the windows in the Embassy's library, which also served as our classroom.

Tamara was serious with her teaching, as long as I didn't touch on any subject that could be interpreted as hurling criticisms at the Soviet Socialist System. She would launch fierce counter-attacks if I did. Sometimes when I wasn't in the mood to study, or when I needed a break, I would raise a provocative statement, like when I said that Soviet-made cars were horrible. That's it. One day, I almost caused her a heart attack when I criticized on the failure of the Socialist system, and I anticipated that Communism would collapse towards the end of the century. Apparently, the staunch Party supporter cried, and I really regretted for the provocation that I had made.

I never missed my class with her during my four-year stay in Moscow, and I would never be able to repay her for the knowledge that she imparted to me. She was not only teaching the language, but also exposing me to the rich Russian literature. I used to translate Russian short stories from famous Russian writers which were published in *Dewan Sastera*[12] magazine back home. Thanks to Tamara for nurturing my interest in that field. After I received a Diploma from Pushkin Russian Language Institute, I still continued my private tuitions with Tamara till the last day of my stay in Moscow.

---

[12]   *Dewan Sastera* is a magazine published by Dewan Bahasa dan Pustaka, Kuala Lumpur, Malaysia.

When I returned to Moscow in 2003, I called my now-retired teacher to say hello. She was so pleased to hear me speaking like a Muscovite. She thought that I would have forgotten the language, after long years of absence from Russia. I hope the Russian government would take good care of her for the loyalty and the service that she had rendered for the country.

Chapter 7

A Student Life at Pushkin Russian Language Institute

fter a year of attending private tuition with Tamara, I could speak a little Russian. I later decided to attend a formal course at the Pushkin Institute of Russian Language. I think I progressed the slowest compared to other students who came from all over the world; from Cuba, Nicaragua, El Salvador, Vietnam, Yugoslavia, Yemen, India, Australia, Brazil, Ethiopia, Zimbabwe, Kenya, (I just mentioned those who were close to me). Tamara would help me catch up with them.

I came to the Institute in the morning in my three-piece suits, and drove a Mercedes Benz (though it was an old car that I bought from the Embassy's auction, it gave such a grand impression). Therefore, I stood out among other students who mostly came from poor socialist countries. They were dependent on the meagre scholarship from the Soviet government. The students were very poor and I always took pity on them. However, the black students from the African countries were living luxuriously, as most of them were engaged in racketeers and black market activities, such as selling electronic goods and imported clothes.

During weekends, I would take some of my classmates from the Institute for a dine-in in some restaurants, as their scholarships were just sufficient for their basic needs. In one occasion, we went to the famous *Arbat* restaurant.[13] It was a crowded place, as the Russians were celebrating Victory Day. It was also a turbulent period, as the Soviets were experiencing a small taste of freedom under Gorbachev's *glasnost* (openness) and *perestroika* (reconstruction) policies. The normally "tame" citizens, especially the youngsters would suddenly became unruly wherever they got together. They fought in restaurants, at football matches, and in rock concerts. Their wild instincts would surface, like caged wild animals that were kept for so long, that when they were released in the open, all hell broke loose. It is human nature I guess. Perhaps they were similar to some cases of Singaporean drivers who were disciplined and well-behaved while in their country. However, the attitude changes as soon as they enter Malaysian territory, and they would treat the highways as Formula One circuit, while throwing empty cans out of the car windows.

At the restaurant, we were trying to avoid from stepping on someone's foot while dancing, as to evade trouble. After less than 15 minutes, fights broke out in the restaurant. We took cover by running back to our table. The fights continued to break up once in a while. Most of the patrons were highly intoxicated, and their brain cells were no longer functioning.

I was just sitting at the table most of the time to avoid any potential trouble. But then trouble came up to me. A

---

[13]   *Arbat* is a famous and oldest streets in Moscow.

drunken youth who walked with the help of a walking stick, approached my table and stared at my colleagues and me. We didn't pay attention to him, as he came close to the table. The youth took my cigarette and put it in his pocket. I tried hard to convince myself that it was not worth it to start a fight over a packet of cigarette. So, I digressed, and let him have it. Then the drunkard went off to disturb another table. They avoided his provocation by going to the dance floor. My blood was boiling for just observing his antics.

Apparently, he returned to our table, and all of a sudden, he tried to fondle and kiss one of my female classmates. I couldn't remember what exactly happened. I later realized that my right hand was holding his throat while my left hand was blocking his walking stick. The drunkard's friends rushed to the scene and pulled him away from me. Instead of joining the fray, they apologized for the guy's action. Apparently, they had been watching the guy's behaviour for quite a while, and blamed him for the trouble.

My other male colleagues who were dancing also rushed to break up the scuffle. Fearing for our safety, the Restaurant Manager came over and politely advised us to leave the place, as he was sure that the trouble maker would return. I refused to leave but my friends pleaded for me to get out of the place as soon as possible. Once outside the restaurant, I protested and wondered why we should be afraid, as the five of us could give them a hard time. Only then Julio, my closest friend from Sao Paolo told me that he was not scared if it was meant to be a fair fight, but then he saw a gun tucked in the guy's belt, as he lifted his hand to swing his walking stick at me. In that case, we made a wise decision to leave the place. It was a lawless, Wild Wild West territory.

The Police came with either three or four large trucks, 10 minutes before the restaurant was closed. They picked up the hooligans, threw them into the truck, and drove them to the station. By that time, they were already too drunk to fight back. It is dangerous to take on a man at the early stage of his intoxication, as he was fearless and couldn't feel the pain inflicted on him. One evening, in a restaurant at Stavropol Hotel in Moscow downtown, I had floored a guy twice, once with a borrowed champagne bottle. The second time was with a solid jab right on his nose. The guy kept rising onto his feet, and charged towards me like an injured bull, as he was bleeding profusely from the wounds on his skull. I had to run for my life. It seemed that I could never cause any pain on that fearless drunkard.

A Policeman friend told me that in the early years of *Perestroika*[14], all lock-ups at the Police Stations around Moscow were full of troublemakers and lawbreakers. I witnessed an incident where a group of youths were chasing and kicking a Policeman who tried to prevent them from gambling on the pedestrian walk. In normal occasions, such an incident was an unimaginable thing to have.

As students, it was compulsory for us to undergo a HIV test. To our surprise, one of our Brazilian friends (it wasn't Julio) from the group has been tested positive and was subsequently sent home. I wish that one day I would bump into some of my classmates from Pushkin Institute of Russian Language, and catch up with old stories.

---

[14] *Perestroika* is the policy of economic and governmental reform instituted by Mikhail Gorbachev in the Soviet Union during the mid-1980s.

Chapter 8

Professor Boris Parnikel

While talking about language and literature, my story would not be complete if I didn't make a mention of Professor Boris Parnikel. Almost every staff at Dewan Bahasa dan Pustaka (DBP)[15] in the late 90s' would remember Pak Boris; a Russian scholar who has translated numerous Malay Classics such as *Hikayat Hang Tuah*[16] *and Sejarah Melayu*[17] into Russian language. Pak Boris, as he was popularly addressed, had mastered *Hikayat Raja Ali Haji* or *Tuhfatul Nafis* better than some of Malay Studies graduates, as he had conducted in-depth research in the subject.

---

[15] Dewan Bahasa dan Pustaka (DBP) or Institute of Language and Literature is the government body that responsible for coordinating the use of the Malay language in Malaysia.

[16] *Hikayat Hang Tuah* is a famous Malay epic connected to the Sultanate of Malacca in the 15th century. It is an epic that tells the story of Hang Tuah, the warrior ever dedicated and loyal to his king, the Sultan of Malacca.

[17] The *Sejarah Melayu* or Malay Annals is the famous and best classical Malay prose. It chronicles the establishment of Malacca sultanate.

I met Boris Parnikel at the gathering of the Association of the Malay Language and Literature in Moscow. He was the President of the Association. He invited me to give a speech on any subject of choice that is related to the Malay language, or culture, or anything in general, since it was an impromptu invitation for me to share my input from behind the rostrum. I spoke about some traditional Malay values, norms and practices. It must have left a lasting impression to the audience, as I could no longer escape from any of their activities after that.

Boris Parnikel revealed to me that he had studied the Malay language, and conducted researches on the Malay literature for more than 27 years. Ironically, he had never stepped foot on the Malay soil. In actuality, the Professor was banned from travelling abroad, after he took part in a poem recital assembly, in commemoration of the controversial Russian writer Boris Pasternak. His revelation prompted me to convince visiting Professor Dato' Ismail Hussain, our national laureate in literature, to work out something for the Russian scholar to visit Malaysia. A big thank you should be given to Professor Ismail, as through his recommendation, Boris Parnikel was offered a job by Dewan Bahasa dan Pustaka (DBP). If memory serves me right, he was offered to conduct some research works for two years. Boris Parnikel returned to Moscow to take care of his ailing mother upon the completion of his contract. After his mother passed away, Pak Boris came back to Malaysia upon invitation by University of Malaya[18] as a Research Fellow.

One week after receiving the good news that he could visit Malaysia, Boris Parnikel was admitted at a hospital,

---

[18]   Universiti Malaya or UM is the oldest university in Malaysia.

and had to undergo a major operation. When I visited him before the surgery, he told me about the bad luck that had befallen him, as after years of dreaming to visit the Malay land, he was facing the prospect of death, or being rendered a cripple before he could realize his dream.

A miracle happened after that. The professor recovered from the critical operation on his spinal back-bones without any serious effects. I remembered his story about faith. He told me that he was originally a free-thinker, as he didn't believe in God. However, when he was in coma, he was visited by a figure in a white dress, which he presumed was an Angel. Since that moment, he believed that there is God. A month after he recovered from the operation, I dispatched him to Kuala Lumpur. Boris Parnikel kissed the ground at Subang International Airport[19] when he stepped out of the terminal.

When I was posted back to Kuala Lumpur, I visited Pak Boris. It seemed that he was enjoying every single moment working at DBP. I visited his rented flat at Pandan Indah, where he proudly showed me a special kind hat that is normally used by explorers while travelling in their research missions. It was hard for him to believe that one day he could own the hat, as it was not available in Russia. He was so happy to have the hat, that one could liken his expression to a guy who was extremely excited to finally own his dream car.

---

[19] Before the opening of the KL International Airport (KLIA) in Sepang, the (then) Subang International Airport   served as Kuala Lumpur's main airport. Subang Airport was renamed Sultan Abdul Aziz Airport and currently serves as   the hub for Berjaya Air, Firefly and Malindo Air commercial turboprop services, as well as for private jets.

One day, a Chinese businessman was looking for a Russian-speaking translator to assist him to understand some findings made by Russian geologists that he hired. The job was in the deep jungle in Raub, Pahang[20]. After the businessman agreed to pay RM500 fees, I requested Pak Boris to accompany me there. We travelled in a bullet-proof 4WD. I didn't know it was a dangerous mission. We arrived at the destination long after midnight to find a few Russian geologists in the deep jungle of Malaysia. Apparently, they were hired by the businessman to find gold reserves. The Russians were trying to tell the Chinaman that they found traces of minerals, which indicated a small amount of gold dust could be found in the area. But the mineral was not concentrated at one place, thus it was uneconomical to mine the gold. I split the RM500 translation fees with Boris. He took the opportunity of the long journey to lecture me on my laziness to continue with what I had started; translation of Russian literature into Malay.

In 2003, I returned to Moscow as the Director of Tourism Malaysia for the Moscow Office. I met Boris a couple of times. The last meeting was when we invited him for National Day Reception held at the Embassy. After the reception, I booked a taxi for him, as I could not send him home. I also slipped two hundred dollar notes in his pocket despite his strong rejection, as I knew it was a difficult time for the old man. A few weeks later, he passed away at the age of 76. I attended his funeral and wrote an article attributed to him, whose contribution to the development of Malay Language and Literature in Russia was enormous.

---

[20] Raub is one of the oldest towns in Pahang, Malaysia and has a long history as gold mining site.

The article was published in *Dewan Sastera* in September 2004 issue.

Despite his death, the specialist doctors who treated Boris remarked that the man had experienced a "miracle". In 1987, Boris Parnikel was found to have suffered from cancer in his blood, and those specialists predicted that the longest period he could survive was 5 years. However, Boris Parnikel lived a full life until he passed away in 2004, thus baffling cancer specialists in Moscow. They jokingly told me, that perhaps Malaysia had given a powerful remedy to the man to fight the disease.

As a close friend, he never told me that he was suffering from cancer. He had never shown any sign of depression. He was always a happy and jovial person. Instead of telling me about his illness, he would only talk about his research works. At the funeral, one of his close associates, Professor Tatiana Dorofeeva (passed away in 2012) told me that a few hours before Boris Parnikel passed away, he gave instructions to have his latest research works to be published as soon possible, as he was ready to work on a new subject. I guess his love and devotion to his work had made him forget about his imminent death.

Pak Boris reminded me about the meaning of humanity and compassion, as well as the beauty of modesty. He lived his philosophy through his actions in his daily life. He had never made an enemy of anyone, nor felt humiliated or angry at any unfair treatment or oppression that he encountered in his life. Although he was sidelined by a less eligible colleague; a person who used dirty tactics to be promoted to Head of Department at his workplace, he never complained nor allowed it to affect the quality and productivity of his work.

Chapter 9

The Encounter

A t one of the receptions organized by the Foreign Ministry, I realized that a tall, smartly-dressed gentleman in his late 20's had been observing me with great interest. I pretended not to notice him, but from his demeanour, I was pretty sure soon that he would approach me sooner or later.

"My name is Victor Kharlamov. I am a journalist from TASS agency".

I looked at this supposedly poor Russian journalist who was presenting himself with a fine double-breasted imported suit. Anyway, instead of disclosing my little thought of him being a potential KGB agent, I gladly accepted his friendly gesture.

Victor Kharlamov was a well-built handsome man. He was about six feet tall, and was always smartly-dressed every time I met him. Even in summer when other people wore casual clothes, he would put on a blazer. Perhaps his act was to conceal his weapon, because there was one time when he came with a long sleeved shirt with a necktie no jacket, while he carried a leather handbag. What he carried attracted my attention. Victor blushed when I jokingly asked if I could have a look at what he was keeping inside the beautiful handbag.

He spoke reasonably good English, but he was too careful in selecting his words. For a secret agent, I could say that he was a little amateurish, as he had the habit of analysing what I have said on the spot. He should have done the analysis in his office. As such, he would pause for a few seconds in deep thoughts after I had said something. A few minutes of silence visibly disrupted the flow of the conversation, but it gave me the opportunity to think of what I would say next. It was always a one-way traffic. He would be the one who asked questions, and I would end up answering them. It was an interview-like conversation. I guessed it was another careless approach done by this young KGB spy.

I sensed Victor was a spy the very first day I met him. He claimed to be a journalist, and yet he was often dressed in imported suits like one of the privileged lot. He spoke English, which is funny, as it's hardly impossible for one to find English, French, Mandarin or Arabic speaking journalists in those days, unless they were the undercover agents. But the main reason why I suspected him to be the KGB officer was through his questions. They were too specific, and in most cases, they were not related to the present issues of which any real journalist would be interested in. In addition he had also shown great interest in me. There were hundreds of other foreigners at the receptions that we attended, but Victor would still be looking for me and kept me company the whole evening. I could no longer run away from him, so I opted to play along with his game. For almost four years, Victor Kharlamov became part of my life, and my shadow.

Sergei S was one of my most trusted Russian friends. He was preparing to defend his PhD thesis when I met him. He did not believe in the socialist economic system. He told me that it was such a painful act when he had to defend and praise the system that he hated so much, in order to obtain his Doctorate in economy. Sergei later became a multi-millionaire as soon as Russia embraced the free market economic system.

One day, Sergei approached me with an alarming look as I was taking an evening stroll in the park near my apartment. He dragged me by the arm, and told me that I had committed a grave mistake.

"Don't you know that you just had lunch with a KGB agent at the Belgrade Hotel!", he screamed.

He didn't feel satisfied when he saw that I wasn't impressed or shocked by his revelation. I asked Sergei on how to confirm that the guy was a KGB agent. He taught me a simple trick as a way to be certain if Victor Kharlamov was indeed a spy.

So, during the following lunch at the Intourist Hotel (Victor would only choose a private room either at the Belgrade, or Intourist Hotel for our "clandestine" meetings), it was confirmed that Victor Kharlamov was indeed a Soviet spy. After the main course, when the waiter came in to take away our plates, I took out a camera from my jacket, and handed it over to the waiter, and asked the guy to take our photo. Victor was caught by surprise, and experienced the biggest shock of his life. He tried to cover his face, when the waiter was focusing the camera at us. As soon as I said that I needed the photo for a competition organized by the US Embassy entitled "Me and My Russian Friend", Victor jumped from his seat, grabbed the camera from the waiter's hand, and chased the poor fellow out of the room. A few seconds later, he was so pale that it seemed he had encountered a ghost, but his face later turned red with anger. When he regained his composure, he tried to give me some lame excuses, like he was camera-shy, his superstitious tendencies, and etc. I quickly changed the subject, and tried to make him forget the incident. But I think he will never forget the incident. Just imagine if his photo is displayed at the wall of the US Embassy, he will definitely be sent to Siberia for his carelessness!

A week before my final departure for home in September 1989, Victor Kharlamov arranged a meeting at a private apartment. He came with another man, whom he introduced as his superior officer, Colonel S. At that meeting, Victor revealed that his rank was a Major, and the Desk Officer for Thailand and Malaysia. Apparently, the revelation came in exchange with my assistance to solve a puzzle, which had been troubling them over the past few weeks.

When Ambassador Renji Sathiah (Dato) went back to Kuala Lumpur for a holiday, the Counselor, AMN (now retired Ambassador) was made the Charge d' Affaires (CDA). The latter took the opportunity to test his strange curiosity. One of Gorbachev's "glasnost" or "openness" policies was to initiate a historic meeting between CIA Chief and his KGB counterpart. It was an unthinkable act during the Cold War period. Indeed, the meeting did manage to take place, and I wondered what had struck AMN, in his capacity as CDA, as he dispatched an Official Note to the Foreign Ministry, and requested for a meeting between him and the KGB Desk Officer in-charge of Malaysia.

The Note had caused panic among the KGB and Foreign Ministry Officials. When Ambassador Renji returned to

Moscow, he ticked AMN for sending such an absurd note. On his part, AMN justified that if the Russians could accommodate a request for a meeting between the top American Spy and the KGB Chief, why couldn't he be given the opportunity to meet his KGB colleague? AMN must have envied me now when he learned that I managed to meet a KGB Desk Officer and his boss without having to dispatch any Note at all!

As I explained the whole scenario about AMN and his Note to the MFA, as his simple way to test the Soviet Union's "glasnost" policy and the Ambassador's reaction to his "unsanctioned" Note to Victor, I could see that his boss was listening attentively without blinking his eyes.

"Are you sure AMN is not working for other intelligent services?"' asked Victor.

Without hesitation I denied that suggestion.

"Then why did he visit US Embassy every week?", demanded Victor.

". . . . because the Foreign Ministry did not provide heated swimming pool for us! That's why AMN had to take his son for a swim at the US Embassy", I quipped.

We had a good laugh at the whole incident. Colonel S told me that for the past three weeks, they had been cracking their heads with all theories and possibilities about AMN's Note to MFA.

At the end of the engagement, Victor surprised me with a special gift; scuba-diving gears. How sweet of him! He must have discovered that over the past few months, this young Malaysian guy had visited all of the sports shops around Moscow to look for diving gears. I intended to take it home, as diving gears in Malaysia would be costly.

I used to think that it was a mere exaggeration when people said KGB knew everything. However, after Victor's open revelation about his identity, he continued to surprise me with many stories about what they knew of my every movement over the past four years. I also learned from him of the many conquests and rendezvous pursued by the Malaysian Embassy staff during their stay in Moscow. The KGB also knew about the covert "*halal* meat operation", but apparently they didn't want to upset us and spared Abdul Haq of trouble. Once, the local Police in Domodedovo summoned Abdul Haq for a brief interrogation about his contacts with some foreigners. However, Victor called up the local Police Chief, and ordered him to release the old man.

During those days, every diplomatic staff and high profile expatriate would be assigned with two KGB Officials to monitor their every movement. The two would have unlimited resources, and "assistants"; the security personnel guarding our apartments, the local staff at our offices, our maids, the shop attendants, hotel managers, restaurant waiters, AEROFLOT ticketing clerks, your music teacher and so forth.

This is a story just to prove my point. In summer 1987, I met a beautiful *debushka* (young lady) at a friend's birthday party. She invited me to see how she lived. Only three months later, when the autumn leaves started to fall that I accepted the offer; an act that I did, after doing some homework on how to get to her place undetected. I drove my old Mercedez Benz to a Kino Theatre near her apartment block, before queuing up to buy the movie ticket. I entered the cinema with the rest of moviegoers, but slipped out from the exit door, walked for another two blocks, before quietly sneaking into her flat. She served me dinner. She presented me with an amber pendant, which I remarked was such a beautiful piece of nature at work (as I could see a small insect was entrapped inside the amber stone). I took out a USD 50 note as payment for the pendant (it was a big sum at that time in the black market) but she refused the money. Instead she asked for a small favour. I left her flat about 2 hours later when the movie ended.

During one of the revelations from Victor about our exploits, he suddenly asked about a young girl named Kristina. I could not remember the girl at all, despite all the various leads that Victor gave; pretty, tall blonde, and a birthday party. They all looked the same, and besides, I had attended so many parties. When he was certain that I really couldn't recall the event, Victor gave me the (catch) clue; the portable washing machine.

Oh my gosh! Only then, I remembered the girl (Kristina) who told me that she didn't need the money, but she would appreciate it if I could get her a portable washing machine that was only available at *BEREOZKA* shop; a special shop to cater for expatriates and where the locals was never allowed to enter.

I accused Victor of "planting" the girl but he insisted that they (KGB) didn't know about her before that. You see, the KGB rank-in-file staff would randomly analyse the list of items purchased by certain diplomats or high profile expatriates from special hard currency shop *BEREOZKA*. That was how they discovered that I had purchased a portable washing machine. When he mentioned about this to the boss, it caught his attention greatly, and raised a question on why I need a portable washing machine, when I already had a good heavy-duty one at home! The instruction was made for the matter to be investigated. The KGB traced the famous 50 dollar washing machine to Kristina's apartment. I only met the girl once and never returned to her apartment again (she was pretty but lacked charming qualities, and I found out that her cooking lacked spices!).

Once, during Victory Day Holiday, I decided to visit the famous Lake Baikal. During The Cold War, the Soviets did not publish the vast lake in their map due to strategic purposes. I boarded a small turbo-propeller Russian plane Antonov 24. After five hours of scary flight, as the small plane seemed to shake easily due to the strong wind, we finally made a stop-over in Ufa, the capital city of the present day Autonomous Republic of Bakhorstan, or formerly known as Bashkiria). We were supposed to be transferred into a bigger aircraft, but unfortunately, the intended aircraft wasn't available at that time. The small plane then headed for a Siberian city, Novosibirsk. But again we failed to board a better plane. The airport workers must have got drunk over the weekend due to Victory Day celebration. After a long wait, the pilot finally decided to continue the flight to Irkurts (capital of Buryatia Autonomous Republic), a city located on the shore of the Great Lake Baikal.

Altogether, we spent more than 18 hours on the journey which would normally take less than 8 hours. Throughout the long flight, we were only served with carbonated water. We were starving and started to protest, but the air stewardess said she was starving too, and so were the pilot and co-pilot. She offered us some vodka if we wanted any.

Safe from the hectic journey, I encountered a serious problem at the hotel counter. Having acknowledged that I had made the booking through the Service Bureau of the Diplomatic Corps, the Manager of Irkursk Hotel however, told me that I didn't have a special visa in my passport to visit Irkursk, so he couldn't give me the room. Apparently hunger had overwhelmed me. I screamed on top of my voice that I had travelled for more than 18 hours, and was only served with carbonated mineral water, and it didn't help that now he was questioning about the bloody visa. I banged the front desk table with my clenched fists. I must have made good use of all Russian foul phrases that I learned before, to the extent that the Manager's jaw dropped, and his eyes kept blinking in bewilderment.

In a matter of five seconds, a stranger softly tapped my shoulder and enquired what the fuss was about. I explained the problem to him. Having examined my documents, he then gestured me to follow him. He took me to a restaurant at the hotel, and told the waiter to quickly bring me some food. He told me to not go anywhere, and he would return to me soon. The man took along my passport, and before leaving, he instructed a colleague sat at the restaurant entrance to watch over me.

As I finished my meals, the gentleman returned with another man who politely asked if I had had a good meal. Now I managed to muster a smile. As anticipated, he was the KGB Chief in Irkursk. We started to discuss about the issue of the special visa requirement. I told him that I was not aware about the requirement for a special visa to visit Irkursk. I started to make cynical comments that I was not aware of the fact that the Soviets had stationed ballistic missiles in Lake Baikal, and that the city was gazetted a "closed" territory. I stated that I was just an ignorant person, and heard so much about the beauty of Lake Baikal, and decided to see it for myself. I haven't in anyway had any intention to threaten the security of the Soviet people, and told them that if they didn't want me to be there, then I would go away the next morning. However, I appealed to the KGB Chief to allow me to stay for the night at the hotel. I suggested that they put a few men to guard my door the whole night, so that no Soviet girls would be able to sneak-in and pass some secret information, and they did. When I took a short stroll at the shore of Baikal in front of the hotel in the evening, a few men can be seen to follow me from a distance. I felt like I was the main character in a James Bond movie, and remembered the song "From Russia with Love" as I sat at the shore of the famous lake, feeling amused.

Actually, they treated me nice as a guest, despite all the insults and cynical remarks that I made. The following morning, the first gentleman who approached me came to the hotel, and drove me to the train station. He waited, until the train left the station before leaving the station for his office. I guessed he waited till the very last minute, in order to write his report and telex an instruction to Ulan Ude station at the border town which could read something like; "The wild monkey just boarded the train. Ensure necessary surveillance measures at your end, and extend your report to Centre".

I jumped into the Trans-Siberian train heading for Ulan Bator, the Mongolian capital. Only then I realized how beautiful Lake Baikal was, as the train wound its way along its shores. The spectacular panorama was graced with bright colours of autumn leaves.

When I returned to Moscow, to my amazement, the first person to call me was this particular "journalist", Victor Kharlamov. I wondered how on earth could a TASS journalist knew so quickly about what had happened to me in a faraway Siberian city. He appeared to be a bit annoyed that I had travelled to a "closed city" without permission. He advised me to be more careful in my adventures, and offered his assistance in arranging for my future trips. From that moment, I knew that I could not run away from this guy, and that I must be extra careful in my activities.

For a certain reason, Victor Kharlamov and the KGB had shown a significant interest in me, despite the fact (which I came to know later) that they had already gained the most valuable and strategic asset in their control, whom they had been blackmailing over the years. I did ask him why they followed me everywhere, knowing very well that I wasn't a spy, and that I will never betray my country nor work for them, or would I intend to do any harm to the Soviet people. He agreed with the first and second points but they simply could not take any chance on the third possibility. Victor said that other intelligent organizations would be pleased to recruit people like me, and he was hoping that I would not betray our friendship.

I was extremely careful in my dealings with Victor. My objective was to convince him that I was not a threat to Soviet Union in any way, and I was not involved in any activities that were against the law. It seemed that I could not run away from him. Therefore, I assured him that I would not be dragged into KGB's traps, or expose myself to blackmails, or land myself in difficult situations. In this respect, I would never turn down Victor's invitations for lunch or dinner, but I remembered well that I had never accepted his offer for a rendezvous with any Russian dolls. Victor would show me photographs of pretty young girls, and said that these particular women would like to meet me for some fun. Sometimes he was so persistent that I agreed to accept the date. However, at the allocated time, I would find strong excuses to skip it, such as having the need to organize the Embassy's family outings in the suburb, or my wife would become suspicious and would start to follow me everywhere the whole day; much to his disappointment when we met at the following meeting. After a couple of times that I bolted out, he realized that this tactic would not work on me.

Anyway, no matter how good they were, as human beings, they made some errors too in their line of duty. Victor made a few wrong assumptions about me. I would like to share one incident of his misjudgement about my rendezvous. One day, during a heavy snow fall, a woman flagged down my car to ask for a ride home. As I was heading in the same direction, I gave her a lift. I came to know that she was Alla Surikova, one of the renowned film directors at MOSFILM[21]. We became friends, and in the following summer, she took me to her countryside home. Once, she took me to the premier presentation of her new film *Two Arrows* where she introduced me to the leading actress in the film, Olga Kabo.

At one of my outings with Victor Kharlamov, he asked me if I had any special relationship with Olga Kabo. Victor must have thought that Olga who used to call me was the celebrated artist. Sheesh! This guy had never stopped listening to my phone conversations. I used the opportunity to boost my ego and let him think that I had been dating the famous actress. Actually, the real Olga was a countryside girl who had hitched a ride in my Suzuki 4WD, when I was heading for a swim at Moscow River over the weekend. She begged me to buy her a pair of imported jeans; a prestigious item but was scarcely available in those days, and she kept calling me for it. We may laugh at them but today, Russians are the most fashionable people in the world. They used to envy my little Suzuki 4WD, but today they are toying around in the latest version of the HUMMER trucks.

---

[21] Mosfilm is a centre for film production for Russia, similar to Hollywood in USA.

Ironically, once we were so afraid of the Russians, and treated them as our adversary. But today, we purchased Russian-made jet fighters and other fire powers to protect our security.

The KGB, having changed its name to FSB, has undertaken new roles after the Cold War, like combating organized crimes, and monitoring international terrorism.

Chapter 10

Riding the Trans-Siberian Train

A mbassador Renji presented me a book that was written by Paul Theroux[22] entitled *Riding the Iron Roaster*. Having read the book, it encouraged me to take the famous Trans-Siberian Train. So, during a summer holiday, I decided to take the trip. I called a colleague in Beijing, and informed him that I would be going in a week's time.

It was an exciting experience in the beginning, as I enjoyed the beautiful panorama of the Russian countryside. I saw simple Russian homes and villages, vast land filled with collective farms, and the so-called the Glory of Socialism. It was a far cry from the homes of farmers in Holland that I witnessed, while taking a train from Amsterdam to Paris.

---

[22] Paul Edward Theroux is an American travel writer and novelist, whose best known work of travel writing. His novel, *Riding the Iron Roaster* is about his travelling experience through China in the 1980s. One of his aims is to disprove the Chinese maxim, "you can always fool a foreigner". It won the 1989 Thomas Cook Travel Book Award.

Suddenly I remembered POTEMKIN, a shrewd Russian aristocrat serving "Catherine the Great"[23] during the Tsar period. When Tsarina "Yekaterina", as it was pronounced by the Russians, wanted to inspect her subjects by taking a boat ride along the Moscow River, Potemkin instructed the villages fronting the Moscow River to be decorated with a beautiful façade. Then, he would select chubby women to be dressed up in colourful costumes. They would be lined up along the river to greet the Tsarina. She would then returned to Kremlin, feeling satisfied that her subjects were living a decent life. Now we are using the "Potemkin act" as a phrase to describe an act of painting rosy picture to cover unpleasant reality. I guessed the Russian countryside was too vast for the Communist Party leaders to put up a Potemkin's show.

After the second day, I began to feel tired and restless for just sitting and looking outside the window. This time I took a single cabin, to avoid a repeat of the incident that happened to me during my last trip on this train from Irkursk to Ulan Bator. Previously, I thought it would be interesting to have a travelling companion, thus prompting me to take a twin-sharing cabin. Apparently, the guy's foot was so smelly that I almost had a migraine. In the end, I spent most of my time sitting along the passage way, to avoid the stinking smell until the train arrived at Ulan Bator. He must have worn his socks for weeks without washing them.

---

[23] Yekaterina Alexeevna or Catherine II, also known as Catherine the Great, Empress of Russia, was the most renowned and the longest-ruling female leader of Russia, reigning from July 9 [O.S. June 28] 1762 until her death at the age of sixty-seven

Later, I finished reading a few books that I took with me, and wondered around from coach to coach, while not knowing what to do next. After three days, the train reached the Russian-Mongolian border. Then, at one place, the train halted, and we were locked inside the cabin. The workers began to change the train's wheels, as the Chinese railway tracks were slightly smaller than the Russian tracks. At first, I thought the engineers of the two communist states were foolish enough not to consider the elements of uniformity and standards for the sizes of their railway tracks before constructing them, but soon I realized that it was by design. Should the two countries enter into a war, the different size of the tracks would delay the opponents from delivering logistic supports to their fighting men.

The job to change the wheels took more than an hour, and my inflated bladder was about to burst. The workers locked the toilet to avoid anyone sending showers of urine on them, as they were working underneath the wagons. As I couldn't stand it any longer, I did it in the tea glass. Now, my problem was how to get rid off the foul-smelling "chemical". The Border Guards locked the doors on both sides of the car; otherwise, I could have found some opening in the area between coaches to empty the glass.

As the workers were changing the wheels, the whole car was shaking and jolting, and I was worried that the foul liquid would spill all over my cabin. I had no choice but to place the glass on the floor of the passage way. There were a few small kids running around in the passage way, and one of them spotted the glass. "*Chai! Cha*i!" (Tea! Tea!) screamed a boy, as he rushed to pick up the glass. I shouted immediately, "*Eto Moi!*" (That's mine!). The startled boy ran back to his mother who gave him a small twist on the boy's ears.

When the train entered Mongolia, the new cabin crew came in. I noticed that there was only one female Mongolian waitress working at the wagon restaurant when I entered for my lunch. She was very occupied in serving tables, as she ran from one table to another. When I demanded to be served, she asked if I came with a tour group. When I said no, she asked me to come back an hour later. So I came back an hour later. Again, she was busy serving another group and sent me away. I came again after another hour, as my stomach was making noisy squeals, but she ignored me repeatedly. This time, the hunger took the better of me, as I screamed at the poor woman,

"What the hell are you doing? Since I travel alone, don't I deserve to be fed? Why don't you dump everything on a plate and give it to me. I promise you that I would be gone in three minutes. But please don't spit on my plate okay!"

I guessed my last words must have amused and softened her heart, as shortly after that, she came out with a tray, and laid it out on the table in front of me with a smile. I gave 10 Roubles as a tip for the waitress, whose salary I estimated was only about 80 Roubles (USD 128 on official exchange rate, but would only worth USD 20 in the black market rate). From that day, she would serve me the moment I entered the wagon restaurant, and prepared the best fruit for my dessert. A couple of months later, I bumped into the Mongolian wagon waitress, while buying a ticket for a circus in Moscow. At first, she couldn't recognize me when I approached her, but she soon remembered when I mentioned about the encounter I had with her in the wagon restaurant. She said she was amused at the episode ". . . please don't spit on my plate . . . .".

The journey was getting tedious for me throughout the Mongolian steppe. The emptiness of the Gobi desert was so dull, and I could occasionally I witness groups of two-humped camels roaming around from time to time. To suppress my boredom, I tried to think about Genghis Khan. It was unthinkable that this barren land had given birth to a great warrior who lived in a "yurt", but managed to conquer mighty kingdoms that were equivalent to half of the world.

I noticed a quiet man in his late 60's who was looking attentively outside the window, and then he noted down something in his book. He had been doing that since he boarded the train in Ulan Bator. My curiosity made me approached him, and I politely asked what he was doing looking outside the window while recording things in his book. He seemed pleased with my presence, and quickly asked if I could help. He told me that he was conducting a research on "Birds of the Gobi Desert", and would appreciate if I could help. First, he described the names of the bird species that flew by, and then told me to count them, as he would record the figures in his inventory book. That way, the job became much easier for him to do, and on my part, I had something to do to kill my time.

I couldn't recall his name, but he wrote down my name, and promised to mention my name in the book that he was planning to publish. The gentleman told me that he had served in the British Army in Malaya before independence when the Colonial was fighting guerrilla warfare with the Communist insurgents. For two days, I helped him with the bird counting. I always invited him to the wagon restaurant for lunch or dinner, but he would politely decline, and told me that he preferred to have his meals in the cabin.

When the train reached the Beijing Station, only then he told me that he was a Courier Officer for the British government, and the person to escort the Diplomatic Bags from the British Embassy in Ulan Bator. Therefore, he could not join me for lunch or dinner, as he was not supposed to leave the cabin unattended. There must be some crucial documents or surveillance reports about the Soviets' activities in nearby regions to the extent that the British had dispatched Her Majesty's Courier Officer to collect the Diplomatic Bags.

When I arrived at the Beijing station, my colleague ZK was already waiting for me. It took me a while to recognise him from the Chinese crowd. Later, I jokingly remarked that he should wear proper attire so that he wouldn't end up looking like a Chinese vegetable seller, which was responded by his trademarked foul language.

During my stay at his house in Beijing, my friend took me around to see the Forbidden City and the Great Wall. He also took me to a State Reception that was hosted by the Chinese government, in honour of Prince Norodom Sihanouk. Before leaving for the reception, I asked my friend repeatedly on the dress code for the evening. He kept saying that casual wear would do just fine. So, both of us put on *batik* shirts[24]. When we arrived at the reception, to my horror, all of the guests were wearing suits, and Prince Sihanouk walked inside the room in his Black Tie! I spent the whole evening in the toilet, and cursed at my friend throughout the entire journey home.

As I was writing this book, Dato' ZK was serving as one of the Department Heads in the Foreign Ministry. He had served as a Malaysian Ambassador to a Gulf State. While returning home for a holiday during a duty tour in Bosnia, he was spotted wearing a pair of striking red shoes. Nevertheless, I considered him as one of the dedicated

---

[24] Malaysian *Batik* is batik textile art of Malaysia, especially on the east coast of Malaysia (Kelantan, Terengganu and Pahang).

Foreign Service officers with good reporting skills; a rare commodity of late.

From Beijing, I took a flight back to Kuala Lumpur to meet my newborn son, Syakir. Having admitted once for surgery for ectopic pregnancy, and having encountered some scary experiences at the Soviet Hospital, my wife would rather leave me alone to 'paint the city of Moscow red' and return home to give birth to our son in Malaysia. Russian hospitals appeared to be a scary place to be in those days. Ironically, today, the Malaysian government sends thousands of its students to study medicine at some Russian medical colleges.

Chapter 11

Gelendzhik and
The Boxing Coach

I n one summer holiday, I decided to accept an invitation
from a Russian Jewish acquaintance, who had earlier
came to the Embassy in Moscow to enquire about
getting a visa to visit Malaysia. He invited me to visit his
hometown Gelendzhik; a small resort town on the North-
Eastern part of the Black Sea. He offered for me to stay at his
home. He came to the Embassy with another friend, Yurie
Lurye, a former boxing coach.

When I arrived at the airport in Krasnodar, I found
out that it was Yurie who was waiting for me, instead of
my Jewish friend. The Jewish acquaintance (whom I could
still remember his face, but not his name) wasn't able to
meet me, as he was receiving visiting relatives. Yurie took
me on a trip through the winding roads to Gelendhik. He
suggested that I stayed at his flat, as the house of the Russian
Jew was crowded with visiting relatives who were coming for
a holiday. I didn't mind putting up with Yurie's flat, except
for the inconvenience and odd situation that I faced at that
time. The former boxing coach was separated from his wife.

However, having no other place to go, she occupied the only bedroom in the flat. I had to sleep in the living room with his son, Stasnislav (Stas), an eight-year old boy, while the host slept on the balcony.

My host expected me to stay for weeks, as the Russians would normally do in summer. However, the crowded beach, plus the summer heat didn't bring me joy. After two days, I grew tired of Gelendzhik, and frantically tried to find my way out of the dull place as soon as possible. I called the Aeroflot Office in Krasnodar, but I was told that all tickets were sold out during the peak summer season. I would have obtained the ticket through different alternative means, if the Airport was nearby. Unfortunately, the distance from Gelendzhik to Krasnodar was about 150 km.

I went to the train station, and checked for trains travelling out of Gelenzhik. The only available train leaving the town would be 5 days later. Nevertheless, I bought the ticket, and continued to endure terrible agony, while waiting for my departure date. The boredom almost drove me crazy. For the first time in my life, I regretted visiting a new place; an act which I would normally cherish. I walked in the woods with Stas, who would follow me everywhere obediently. After some time, Stas, a school drop-out, became a nuisance. I felt deeply sorry for the poor boy who had never let his eyes off me in full admiration.

Galendzhik, as pictured in Lermantov's Novel *Hero of Our Time* (Geroi Nashevo Bremeni) in the episode entitled *Taman*, was portrayed as a mysterious port, where the main character in the novel, a Military Officer, was sent to join the Caucasus Regiment. He stopped for the night at the shore, on his way to Caucasus. There, the Officer witnessed strange activities took place, under the guise of mist and darkness; a blind woman and her companion in the lone boat approached the shore in the wee hours of the morning. At the end of the story, the Officer was hit on the head, and lost consciousness, when he tried to investigate what was going on. Apparently the "blind woman" was in fact a man in disguise who was involved in smuggling activities. The storyline itself was unpleasant. Well, I didn't see any mysterious woman or lonely boat, but the atmosphere of the place was indeed unbearable.

As a matter of fact, Gelendzhik was a beautiful town that was located by the Black Sea. Today, Gelenzhik has developed into a striking and exclusive resort city for the rich and famous. I was unhappy then because of the awkward situation I had.

In that full week, Yurie narrated to me his bitter life story. Once, he was a celebrated boxing coach with the Soviet national team. He had the privilege to travel abroad with the team, with destinations that were mostly to the socialist countries in Eastern Europe and Cuba. These countries are no different from the USSR. However, his experience and fate took a sharp turn after his visit to Singapore. All Soviet officials must write a report every time they returned from overseas trip. The guidelines were as follows; if they visited socialist countries, the report must be carried out together with full of praises for the glory of socialism. But, if the visit was made to capitalist countries, the report must condemn the setbacks of the capitalist system.

Apparently, the boxing coach had fallen in love with Singapore, for he failed to highlight his bad experiences in the tiny island state. Instead, he wrote about the beautiful things about Singapore; the cleanliness, the friendly and happy people, the large shopping malls full of excellent products, good foods, etc. His superiors were obviously not amused, and they made him rewrite another report, of which he refused to do.

Consequently, his superior filed a report to the Politburo Committee, and fabricated the case, saying that Yurie had misappropriated some funds, and they subsequently threw him in jail. Deeply depressed, he cut his vein (the scars were clearly visible on his left wrist) and consequently, they transferred him to a mental institution. When he got out of the institution, his wife filed for a divorce, and he was jobless. He obviously had a strong reason to resent the system.

When I returned to Malaysia, Yurie and Stas came to Kuala Lumpur, and sought for my help to recommend him for a job at the National Boxing Council. But they didn't take him in at the time, as no one in Malaysia with a sound mind would dare to hire a Soviet citizen at that time. Furthermore he could hardly speak English. When his attempt to get a political asylum from the UNHCR office at Jalan Bellamy was turned down (since it could hardly cope with the influx of Vietnamese refugees), I put him on the plane to Bangkok, as per requested by him.

I lost track of him until several years later, when I received a letter from him in Peru, Chile, with the photos of him and Stas. The unkempt little boy has grown to be a tall smart young fellow. The school dropout was also able speaks 7 foreign languages now. What happened was, when the Thai authorities detained them for illegal entry, they were deported back to Soviet Union. Determined to leave the country, they built a small yacht made of waste materials that they gathered around Gelendzhik. They sailed from port to port around the world. In order to avoid any mishaps, as their boat was fragile, they sailed close to the shores. The duo earned a living by offering services to clean and repair boats at marinas that they anchored. When they arrived at the Chilean shores, a big wave hit the dilapidated yacht. It broke down into pieces and capsized. Since then, Yurie and his son Stas have settled down in Peru.

When Yurie managed to re-establish his contacts with me a few years back, and after I had replied to his letter, he made several phone calls from the internet café, and asked if the Malaysian Boxing Team needed a coach. I told him that the Malaysian team had already employed a Kyrgyz trainer, and one of our boxers, Sapok Baki, had won the first ever gold medal for Malaysia at the 1998 Commonwealth Games.

I admired this team of father and son, who braved violent storms and numerous challenges along their way, in their search for happiness. They have shown strong will in pursuing their dreams, and they didn't give up easily. They might never succeed in getting what they wanted in life, but their struggles had made their lives worth living. I was thinking if they were Malaysian citizens, they would end up being bestowed with a *Datukship*[25]. A couple of months ago, I received an email from Yurie. He sent me an article about his bad experience during his trip to Guyana, where he was deceived by the government officials, and ended up penniless and hungry on the street. Finally, he met a kind-hearted person who took him back to Peru on his private jet. Should I have extra money to spend, I would like to go there, and look for Yurie and Stas in Peru. Perhaps, we could buy a yacht and sail around the world after that.

---

[25] *Datuk* is an honorary title conferred since 1965 for outstanding services to the country or great contribution to the society. The title is awarded by His Majesty the King at Federal Level and Malay Rulers at the state level.

Chapter 12

Caucasus, Land of Saints

I woke up very early in the morning on the day of my departure. I didn't want to miss the train, as I really need to leave the dreadful town, before I would end up becoming crazy for overstaying. Yurie had requested his friend who owned a Soviet car, Zhiguli, to send me to the train station. A few days before, I had purchased a one-way ticket to Makhachkala, the capital of Dagestan. Without any plan, I decided to visit a friend, the Deputy Mufti of Dagestan, whom I met at the International Islamic Conference in Tatarstan. I had always wanted to visit this land for a very long time, and perhaps it was the best opportunity to do so.

If the Communists sent criminals and the enemy of the people to Siberia, the Russian Tsars prior to the Socialist Revolution would have undisciplined military officers, plus those who committed various offenses to be thrown to the Caucasus Regiments. Most of them would perish in Caucasus under the Chechens' curved swords or flying bullets. Taking part in the duel had been one of the typical cases for the officers (for those who survived the shootout anyway) to be sent to the Caucasus Regiments. Ironically, the ladies in those days were fantasizing about the officers serving in the Caucasus Regiments. The ladies saw them as brave heroes who risked their lives in defence of their honour. This perception was again beautifully captured in Lermantov's classic novel Hero of Our Time, which is a worthy read.

Another classic writer, Lev Tolstoy (Leo Tolstoy) also wrote many famous stories about the Caucasus. Two of them were entitled Haji Murad and The Cossacks. In real life, Haji Murad was the only remaining two survivors (the other was Imam Syamil) of the Russians' onslaught on a Caucasus fortress. Once, the region was known as "Land of Saints", where many prophets and saints were roaming the land. Imam Syamil was a legendary figure for Dagestan and the Caucasus people. For 25 years, the Great Warrior managed to unite more than 100 different clans who fought each other for decades. For nearly 25 years, Imam Syamil bravely fought the Tsarist Army in the Caucasus, and managed to keep the invading enemies at bay. That was until he fell from grace, when he was betrayed by one of his loyalists.

I read numerous books about the Caucasus people. They were written by old and contemporary writers. A famous Dagestan writer, Rasul Gamzatov who lived during the Communist period, wrote an excellent book entitled My Dagestan which depicted its culture and tradition, as well as the ordinary life of Dagestan people after the revolution. Although he managed to portray the old traditions of the mountain people marvellously, Rasul Gamzatov, being a member of the Communist elites who had been given all sorts of privileges, including a large apartment in Moscow, had fully adopted a Soviet lifestyle. That explains why in his book the writer tried to propagate Soviet's culture in the life of the Caucasus people, such as the mention that vodka drinking should be considered a cherished tradition. Ironically, the taste was much to the dislike of his own natives.

Intrigued by the stories above, I was motivated to visit Dagestan. It took two days by train to reach Makhachkala, the capital town of Dagestan; a place that is located at the shore of the Caspian Sea. Somehow, I managed to call my friend, Kalimullah, the Deputy Mufti, who lived in a remote village up in the mountain. He rushed down to Makhachkala to fetch me in record time, as he said that he was overwhelmed with joy to receive me as his guest.

I was taken along the winding mountainous roads, which has the panoramic view of its land and inhabitants. They were friendly people who offered greetings to each other, irrespective of whether you are friends or strangers. They showed great respect to the elders. I noticed that there was a large number of old people in Caucasus, as I was travelling along the way to Kalimullah's village. He explained to me that mountain people lived longer, as they breathed clean air, eat grains that were grown on uncontaminated soil, and led a simple life, without much to worry about (those were peaceful periods, before the Chechen wars changed the landscape of Caucasus). I guessed that by having to walk up and down the mountain paths daily was also a factor that made them achieve a healthy and long life.

I had yet to arrive at the village, but I had already experienced interesting culture and traditions of the mountain people. When we were passing a graveyard, Kalimullah recited some prayers for the dead. He would repeat the act when he passed another cemetery. After the third cemetery, I asked if he had any relatives buried there too. To my surprise, with a tinge of embarrassment, he told me that he had no relatives whatsoever in all of the three cemeteries that we passed by, and revealed that he gave the prayer to them solely because those were after all his Muslim brothers! There was a teenage boy on a motorcycle, riding in front of us, with a large cargo loaded on his bike. I was astonished to witness his devotion to pray for the dead every time he passed by a graveyard. He would lift one hand to pray, and let the other do the balancing act, as his bike was fully loaded with cargo. All together, there were seven or eight graveyards that we passed that day, before we finally reached Kalimullah's house. More surprises were revealed to me during my one-week stay with Kalimullah's family.

Chapter 13

The Follower of (*Sunnah*) Prophet

Muslims of the Sunni Sect follow 4 Imams; Hanafi, Shafie, Hambali and Malik. Most of the Muslims in Russia and Central Asia were the followers of Imam Malik. To my surprise, Kalimullah informed me that Dagestanis are the strong followers of Imam Shafie. I had already witnessed their devotion to pray for the dead. Malaysian Muslims had always claimed that they are staunch followers of Imam Shafie, but we hardly see people praying for the dead, when we pass by the graveyard, except perhaps once or twice a year, when we visit our the graves of our parents or grandparents during Eid.

At Kalimullah's house, the whole family members, young and old, performed the intricate details of the 'Sunnah; the daily routine or practice of Prophet Muhammad (PBUH) that all Muslim should follow. I could write a few chapters on this, but then, this book would end up appearing like a religious book.

Kalimullah spoke fluent Arabic, and has a vast knowledge of Islam. He never attended any formal religious school, but through his father, he learned all the branches of Islam. The extent of his knowledge was at in the state that he could even discuss and debate freely with graduates from University of Al-Azhar, Cairo on complex issues. When I stayed with him at his domain, I can see how he taught his sons of the Arabic language, and the two of them were already at the advanced stage of Arabic and Islamic studies. These could only be achieved by true dedication, and a strong discipline.

Knowing the knowledge of Islam is one aspect, but fully practising Islamic way of life is another matter. Having witnessed the way of life of this small Dagestani community, I experienced a pleasant "cultural shock" during my stay at Kalimullah's home, and realized how much I had to catch up to be a good Muslim. I was not just referring to the *ibadah* (practice) alone as a yardstick in my evaluation of a "good Muslim", as someone who wakes up in the middle of the night to pray and perform *zikir*[26] till morning is yet to be qualified as a good Muslim.

Kalimullah demonstrated the beauty of refined behaviour and exemplary ethics at all times, and in all situations. He was always soft spoken and smiled when talking to someone, while never vented his anger in any way. He showed great respect and consideration to other people, even to the non-Muslims, and was always nice to the kids. He was proposed by many to become the Mufti because of his shining reputation, and his great level of knowledge of Islam. However, when a few other elderly people were lobbying to occupy the post, Kalimullah stepped aside, and refused to be involved in the squabble for power.

---

[26] *Zikir* or *Zikr* is an Arabic word meaning remembrance to Allah.

Nevertheless, they made him the Deputy, and entrusted him with most of the job, while the Mufti was only performing ceremonial tasks. He didn't complaint nor expressed his resentment to anyone. He never once tried to show off his vast knowledge.

I had a pleasant stay with Kalimullah's family. He took me to visit his relatives and friends in the mountains, to experience the hospitality of the Caucasus natives. Kalimullah also took me to another friend who lived near Caspian shore and worked as an Enforcement Officer in the Fisheries Department. Together, we went out to the Caspian Sea to catch sturgeons. I had witnessed how they slit open a 30-kg fish, and took out the eggs to produce "caviar". Before I left Makhachkala, the friend gave me two kilogrammes of caviar to take home; a delicacy which would have cost a couple of thousands of dollars today.

Kalimullah took me to a Museum in Makhachkala for a compulsory visit to a section devoted to Imam Syamil, the legendary religious leader and warrior. I was so charmed by the charismatic Imam, that I named my third son after him.

From Makhachkala, I went to visit another friend in Grozhny, the capital of present-day Chechnya. My friend, Zelim Khan, was a Mufti of Chechen-Ingushetia. I also met him at the same Islamic Conference in Tatarstan. It was the same venue where I met Kalimullah in the first place. However, the characters of the two Muftis of Caucasus Republics were as different as the heaven and earth. A slender tall Mufti in his 50's, he didn't look like a religious person, but was more of a Chechen jigit or horseman, as he walked around in traditional Chechen costume with a curved dagger dangling from his belt. Zelim Khan spoke in a high commanding, pitched voice like a true warrior.

The Chechen Mufti hardly talked about religious matters. Instead, he asked me whether I was a good horseman (rider). If I could prove to be a real *jigit*, then he would propose that I marry one of the beautiful girls in the village. However, he reminded me to be careful with the Chechen brides, as they always practice a long-lived tradition of hiding curved daggers under the pillow during the wedding night. The bride would strike at her husband once he entered the room with the curved dagger, and would only surrender herself to him, if the husband could overpower her. When I asked about what was the rationale behind it, Zelim Khan told me that if the man could not handle a woman, then how could he be expected to protect the family and his land.

I thanked Zelim Khan for his offer, but said "No" to a Chechen bride. I said to him that in Malaysia, the bride would rush and kiss the husband's hand when he enters the room, before leading him to the soft comfortable bed, where she would entertain the newlywed husband with different songs the whole nightlong, and then be the judge of her husband's prowess.

I only stayed in Grozny for two days. Once, it was such a beautiful place, but today I would shed tears if I visit the place again, as I was told that not a single building survived the Russian bombings during the second round of onslaught on Chechnya. By the way, only a few realized about Moscow's hidden motive for the massive bombings of Grozny. Prior to the event, US-led NATO allies had bombarded Yugoslavia, despite strong objections by Moscow. The bombings of Grozny were to demonstrate the Russian military's mighty prowess, and to gain respect from US and its NATO allies.

I blamed the Chechen leaders for the catastrophe that they brought to their country and the people. Chechnya first waged war against Russia during Yeltsin's era, in its attempt to break away from the Russian Federation. Then, the ceasefire was initiated, when the Chechen fighters gained the upper hand, plus they were strong fighters. Therefore, Chechnya was accorded with maximum autonomy, including the rights for the group to run the country freely without Moscow's interference, except on foreign policy matters, when policies must be in line with Moscow's. They had almost everything they wanted, except to have a sovereign state. The Chechens should have maintained that status-quo, and used the opportunity to develop their country, and remained under Moscow's protection. Sadly, some warlords returned to the old, traditional lifestyle of the mountain people, who once lived to plunder and rob people. They terrorized the streets, and kidnapped foreign workers for ransom, with some were cruelly beheaded, even though they originally came to install the infrastructure for the country. When all foreigners had left, they began to harass their own people. Those warlords made a grave mistake, when they tried to incite some factions in Dagestan to rise against Moscow.

President Putin, who took over from Yeltsin, seized the opportunity to justify Moscow's second invasion that brought the entire country into rubbles. Now, the poor, innocent citizens were caught in between two fighting sides. If they showed sympathy to the Chechen fighters, they would be harassed by the Russian soldiers, and if they didn't take sides, the Chechen fighters would visit them in the middle of the night, and punished them for the betrayal of their struggles.

I used to resent the Russian soldiers who were involved in the genocide of innocent Chechen people. I had seen a video recording of Russian soldiers' cruel treatment of dead Chechen fighters, as they cut the private parts from the dead bodies of Chechen fighters, and stuffed them into the mouth of the dead. However, my perception changed, when I watched another video showing how Chechen fighters treated the captured Russian soldiers. The Chechens lined up captured young Russian soldiers, who were reluctantly enlisted to the battle front in the first place, and slaughtered them like a flock of sheep. Both sides are guilty of the crimes against humanity.

Chapter 14

The Uzbek Land

U zbekistan is blessed with rich natural resources, such as oil and gas, as well as minerals like gold, copper and aluminium. Its fertile land is cultivated with cotton, rice, grapes and other fruit trees and vegetables.

Uzbekistan's capital, Tashkent, located in an oasis, has a long history of being one of the flourished trading centres during the Golden Silk Route period. From the 10th to 18th Centuries, the Central Asia that was known as the land of Turkestan had became the centre of Muslim civilization. The land had given birth to many great scientists and scholars, such as Al Khorezmi (the founding father of Algebra), Abu Ali Ibnu Sina (or Avicenna, the father of modern medicine), Al Beruni, Al Farabi, Alisher Novoii, as well as famous Islamic jurisprudents, such as Imam Ismail Al Bukhori and Al Termizi, just to name a few.

When the country managed to free itself from the Soviet Union, there was high expectation among the people, that the newly elected and independent leadership would bring the country towards a smooth transformation into a progressive, modern nation. There were some encouraging signs in the early 1990's, when Uzbekistan was moving towards market reforms.

However, a couple of years later, as other neighbouring countries progressed ahead, Uzbekistan did not continue with its reform policies. After a few frustrating years of waiting for the changes, most of the investors packed up and left the country. Since this is not a political book, I do not wish to dwell further on the issues related to the country's top leadership, his unpopular policies, and the sorry state of the Uzbek people. In short, what happened to the country could be summarized by the prevalence of high rate of unemployment and hardship of people, when university professors and other professionals such as engineers, lawyers and architects were forced to become private taxi operators.

Chapter 15

Uzbek Hospitality

The Uzbeks are known for their hospitality and good at entertaining their guests. They would choose a nice place at the Ankhor riverbank, and lay out a huge table full of local delicacies. Then, the guests would be served with several course meals, till their stomachs became bloated like huge melons. Normally, the appetizer alone is already too much to take. Pilaf rice[27] would always be the last course. By then, you would already feel lethargic, with the feeling that the stomach would burst due to the excessive food intake.

There was this businessman who was toying with the idea of taking a local woman as his second or third wife. He had swallowed whatever food that was served before him, and when the "pilaf" arrived, he could no longer take it. The host told him that the oily rice was the grand finale for the evening, and he must try it. To inject fun, I had altered the meaning of the conveyed message by the host in my translation. I told the businessman that for a certain

---

27 Pilaf is a dish originated from Middle East and the rice is cooked with lambs or poultry broth.

reason, the Uzbek people judge a man's sexual prowess, by looking at how much a person could consume the pilaf. If the person could eat a great amount of the national dish, he is undoubtedly believed to be strong in bed. But if a man is seen to take little interest in the national dish, then the last thing that they would do is to take him as their in-law. What happened next to the businessman, you can figure it out yourselves, with him almost ended up crawling back to his hotel room.

If you are invited to a dinner at home by the local host, you shouldn't forget to remind your wife that you would be back late at night. Otherwise, she would be thinking that you must have gone for a sauna with someone. The dinner, which normally starts at 8.00 pm, would end slightly just before midnight.

Dinner in Uzbeks' homes is always an all men's affair. It means that you wouldn't find a single female member of the house participating in the feast. Uzbek women are always in the background. Sometimes you feel sorry for them for having to cook all night long in the kitchen.

Once, I was invited to a dinner by a Kyrgyz Senior Official at his residence. I took along a visiting Malaysian Foreign Ministry Official, Dr F. We were treated with a typical Central Asian warm hospitality. However, what made us uncomfortable was the way the man treated his wife. Clapping his hands, he would shout to his wife and ordered her to bring the dishes and clear the food from the table; a situation no different from a master treating his slaves in ancient times. The worst part was that he was proud to show off that he was the master of the house, and was regardless of the humiliation suffered by his poor wife. Later, I learned that he was once married to a Russian woman who refused to be treated in that manner, and consequently dumped him unceremoniously. When he took a new wife from his own people who would submit to his dominance, he lost all of his senses.

Meanwhile, in Kazakhstan, guest of honours would be served a crude boiled sheep's head. Most of the foreign guests would experience the shock of their lives, when the ceremonious dish of boiled sheep's head was taken out and placed right in front of them. It was scary at the first sight to witness the whole head of a sheep, with its protruding teeth grinning at you. As a guest of honour, you are expected to cut the different organs of the sheep's head, and offer them to the people sitting around you. Each organ represents different meaning. The ear should not be given to elders, as the act would offend them. The ear is meant for the children, as they still need to listen to the elders' advice, while the tongue should be offered to the wisest man in the gathering, such as *akin* (highly respected elders in Kazakh community); a suggestive gesture to show that you were ready to listen to their wisest advice. Well, you can still have the eyes, nose, lips . . .

Chapter 16

An Outing with a Lot of Cash

W hen I was instructed to establish a resident
mission in Tashkent (Embassy) in early 1993, we
had to bring a lot of cash for our expenditures.
During our first trip to Tashkent, we had to carry US627,000
dollars cash with us. It was a dangerous thing to do, but
we had no other choice. In those days, the former Soviet
republics (even today in the case of Uzbekistan) did not
have an internationally-practiced banking system. If we
deposited our hard currency in the local bank, we would end
up withdrawing the local currency *Som*, with value that kept
on dwindling in every single minute. Meanwhile, in major
transactions such as house rental, purchase of automobiles
and purchase of electronic items, the service providers or
suppliers would be asking for hard currency, preferably the
US dollars.

Since we were staying at a run-down hotel without
proper security, we had to carry around the cash in a leather
backpack wherever we went. To the extent, we even carried
the backpack to the toilet, when there was no one else in the
room to look after it. At night, my Assistant would use the
backpack as his pillow. When we had to get our provisions

from the Bazaar, someone would walk in front of the cash bag's carrier, while being closely guarded from behind by two trusted male local staff. In one occasion, our local staffs were pulled aside by a civilian-cloth policeman who thought they were snatch thieves who were preying on us.

During a local holiday, some friends invited us to join them for an outing at an oasis, known for its charming tranquillity in Jizzakh region. It was located at a mountain pass between Tashkent and Samarqand. What attracted me to the place was the fact that the sandwiched passes between the rugged terrains had been used by many armies of great conquerors, such as Alexander Macedonian, Genghis Khan, Timurlane, the Arab Commanders and Persian Kings.

We then hired a van, and travelled about 250 km from Tashkent with our cash bag. There were five of us: Shahrom, Nazri, his Kurdish wife, Suham and their young son, Ahmed and I. We were joined by an Uzbek family who arranged the trip for us. After reaching a small settlement and passing by Jizzakh town, our van had to make an exit from the main road, that took us to dusty roads that were ascending to the high grounds. It was indeed a bumpy ride. The area was a semi-arid land with slopes, ravines and rugged terrain. There was no sign of people living nearby, except for a few *chobon* (shepherds) on horsebacks that could seen from afar managing their flocks of fat-tailed sheep.

In about an hour or so, we reached a small stream. The car stopped there, and we tracked the upstream, until we reached a spring that formed a small pond with sparkling, crystal clear water that flowed down, and formed another small stream. Pines, Oaks, Cedars and a few other species of trees were found around the pond. There were a couple of platforms built just above the pond, with mountain trout swimming around the platforms. The wooden platforms were laid with colourful *qurpacha* (large cushion pillows stuffed with cotton) that allowed us to sit comfortably. There were already a few Uzbek families there when we arrived.

The beauty of the place was beyond description. It was a hot summer time, but the mountain spring water and the shades of birch trees had protected us from the excessive heat. We had *shashlik* (traditional Uzbek-style grilled lambs) and various local cuisines prepared by a local woman. She was determined to win my heart so that I would marry her daughter. The long session of eating and feasting on varieties of grapes, peaches and sweetest melons (honey dew) while reclining on very comfortable cushions and pillows had soon gave an affect on us; we became half-awake and sleepy.

Our Secretary, Nazri was the first person to fall asleep, followed by my Assistant, Shahrom. The small boy, Ahmad, was running from one corner, to the other to feed the trouts. When his snoring was getting louder, I carefully lifted Sharom's head, and tried to remove his "pillow" (his cash-filled backpack), while Suham giggled to see the whole thing. However, he opened his eyes and smiled at me, when he realized that I was testing his vigilance.

We stayed at the pond until late evening. I couldn't hide my desire to grab one or two trouts that were tamely swimming in the pond. Apparently, the elders had invented a legend that says whoever catches or consumes the fish, he or she would face an instant death. They told the story in great seriousness and strong conviction, that highly superstitious visitors would be totally convinced by it. They feed the fish and never disturb its habitat, and the trouts continued to multiply in large numbers. I told Shahrom that if we were left alone without the presence of other people, we would have feasted on the best grilled mountain trout for dinner!

We had a good outing, after weeks of running around with a lot of cash, in the process of establishing our diplomatic mission in the capital of Uzbekistan. Thank God we managed to keep the huge amount of cash safe for months, till we had a proper premise to keep the money.

Chapter 17

My Kurdish Little
Sister, Suham

She was born in a prominent business family. However, at the same time, it was unfortunate that she was from a Kurdish clan; an Iraqi minority group that received harsh treatment during Saddam's reign. Another hardship faced by her was when she fell in love with this young male Secretary at The Malaysian Embassy in Baghdad, where she worked as the Locally-Recruited Staff. Suham, a sweet Kurdish young girl, had braved numerous challenges to be with her husband, Nazri, who is now the Senior Personal Assistant at the Malaysian Foreign Ministry (and is currently serving in Havana).

Suham's family had to bribe Iraqi Officials with nearly USD 200,000, to enable her to obtain the passport and exit visa, so that she could follow her husband, Nazri upon the completion of his duty tour in Baghdad. It was a brave decision, as once she left the country, the chances for her to return was very slim. She knew that it would probably be the last time for her to see her parents, brothers and sisters. However, love-stricken, she made a great decision to be with the man, whom she was head-over-heels in love with. Then, the war started in Iraq, and she lost track of her family. When I first met her in March 1993, it was already over 8 years since the last time she was able to contact any of her family members.

When we arrived to establish a resident mission in Tashkent, I was accompanied by our Third Secretary Shahrom, Nazri as the Personal Assistant, his wife Suham, and their 2 year-old son, Ahmed. We had a temporary office in a small hotel, where Shahrom and I stayed, while Nazri and his family stayed in a rented two-bedroom flat. Shahrom and I would go to the house every day for lunch and dinner.

Suham was an intriguing character full of fear that she was on the verge of paranoia. She was afraid of everything; strangers, animals, plus other things, except Nazri and little Ahmed. She confessed that she was scared stiff when she saw me for the first time. However, her perception of me was changed completely, after she knew more of me after that.

My assistant Shahrom could sometime be a funny and mean person. Knowing very well of Suham's character, he would play some tricks on her. The quality of petrol in Tashkent was very poor. It could be detected from the dirty condition of the exhaust pipes of every car in the area. However, the most glaring sign of the low grade fuel was that the exhaust pipes would let out frequent loud explosions. One evening, while we were having dinner, a loud bang from someone's exhaust pipe startled us. Shahrom then casually remarked;

"Akhh . . . . another victim. Today alone, four people had already been gunned down in broad daylight . . . . What is going to happen to this country?" he sighed.

Nazri and I just smiled at the remark, while continued to enjoy our dinner. However, Suham was staring at my face, with eyes that could almost pop out from the sockets. Nevertheless, I didn't sense any alarming sign, as she indeed has a pair of large suspicious eyes. Furthermore, I never expected that Suham would take Shahrom's remarks so seriously, until one day when she asked me why the people in this country were so violent. When I questioned of what made her draw to that conclusion, she simply said,

"Remember that day . . . Mr Shahrom said that four people were shot dead in one day; you heard the gun shot when we were having dinner . . . ."

I burst out laughing, and shook my head in disbelief! No wonder Suham had never ventured outside the flat, even though it was located so close to the pedestrian walk along the Ankhor River, where many people would take a stroll in the evening. She was too scared to go out. Therefore, she spent most of the time in the flat with Ahmed, as we were too busy to set up the Embassy during the first two months.

In one weekend, we followed a local friend to visit his relatives in a remote village that was located about 150 km from Tashkent. As we didn't have any itinerary to follow, we decided to take the opportunity to witness a typical Uzbek village. When we arrived at the village, we saw clear views of poverty that were perhaps similar to the views of some of our rural people and their lifestyle back in the 60's. Children with bulging stomachs were running around without shirts and shoes, and there were shabby houses made of clay bricks, with no running water or other facilities.

Nevertheless, no matter how poor they were, those people tried their best to serve us with maximum hospitality. They slaughtered a sheep for our dinner, and baked fresh round breads from the clay *thandur*, while the daily food for most of them were plain bread or potatoes with tea. Their lives were much better during the Soviet period, with the collective farms.

At night, we converted a large platform under the vines, as our bed and about 12 adults and kids slept together on the same platform. Suham chose her spot in the middle of the platform. The long journey had made us doze off instantly, until we were rudely awakened by Suham's shrieking scream. A dog had sneaked under the platform to find a spot to sleep, which had caused her such havoc. The next morning, she whispered to me that she didn't sleep the whole night, for being totally scared out of her wits.

When we had settled down, Nazri and his family moved into a house a few doors away from our driver's home. One day, as I was passing by it, I remembered that I had to collect something from the house. After a couple of minutes of knocking at the door and buzzing the bell, I became suspicious, when Suham didn't open the door. It was snowing heavily. I peeked through the gate, and saw that Ahmed was running to and fro, as if he was trying to tell something (Ahmed could not speak until he was 4 years old). I climbed the metal gate and to my horror, I saw Suham was lying unconscious in the compound. Her whole body was covered with snow. Her face turned blue in colour. I carried her inside the house, and called her husband Nazri to come home as fast as he could, as I was struggling to fix the oxygen tank[28]. Suham was suffering from chronic asthma, and the attack that day was severe that she lost her consciousness.

---

[28] Oxygen tank is referring to a special machine or equipment used for asthma patient.

She always said that I had saved her life but I said that God still wanted her to live, and it was not me who saved her, but her love for Nazri that gave her the strength to fight for her life. Indeed, her love for her husband was so strong, that she had confessed to me for numerous times that if Nazri were to leave her, she would die. One evening, we gathered at my house for a karaoke session. As I was helping Suham in the kitchen, we heard Nazri's voice imitating Englebert Humperdink

". . . Please release me and let me go . . . for . . . I don't love you anymore . . ."

Before he could finish the next line, Suham stormed out from the kitchen screaming . . .

"What? What? . . . Do you want me to die? Do you really want to see me dead? . . ."

We were laughing at her for being unnecessarily distressed. Apparently she was serious about it as she grabbed the mike and asked Nazri to choose another song.

"Honey . . . Try Love Story, it is a nice song", she suggested.

She was fond of me too. She said that I reminded her so much of one of her favourite brothers. Not that I physically looked like the brother, but the way I talk and move, plus my robust character in particular. Sometimes she would stare at me for a long time and always ended up with tears rolling down her cheeks.

"Hey sister . . . why are you crying over a distant brother? Here I am, so close to you . . ."

Suham had repeatedly said that she would always pray for my happiness. Likewise, my poor little sister, wherever you are. Ahmed must be 17 years old now.

Chapter 18

Malaysian Business Ventures in Uzbekistan

F ollowing the fall of the Soviet Union, Uzbekistan and 13 other Soviet Republics gained their independence. The country's first President, Islam Karimov, then visited Kuala Lumpur in early 1993, this was reciprocated by the Malaysian Prime Minister at that time, Dr Mahathir Mohamed (*Tun*).

Kuala Lumpur decided to establish a diplomatic mission in the Uzbek capital, and started to encourage Malaysian businessmen to explore business opportunities in those newly independent republics.

Malaysian businessmen were coming in droves to Tashkent. Some travelled in style, as the Malaysian economy was booming in the early 90's. I remembered an incident when a Malaysian businessman purchased a few old boats as scrapped metals in one of the African countries, the newspapers back home reported that the businessman had purchased a fleet of ships, thus pushing his share prices up a few points. Those were the days when, some Malaysian businessmen turned their characters for the worse, seemed to have lost their senses, and some even became arrogant in behaviour.

In another instant, a prominent businessman led a group of friends to Tashkent to explore investment opportunities, but a few members of his party went there solely for the fun prospects. They arrived in style with a chartered MAS aircraft[29]. What puzzled us was that the group, which had scores of consultants and managers, failed to do a little bit of research of the capital, before arriving in Tashkent. Instead, without checking the real situation in the country and perhaps, fearing they would be starved to death in this unknown territory, they brought along chefs and kitchen helpers, with supplies of various foodstuff; eggs, flour, frozen meat, cooking oils, vegetables, and etc. In the end, they found out that there was an abundance of spices, fresh meat, vegetables and fruits of highest grades that were available at the Tashkent bazaars at unbelievably cheap price.

When Genghis Khan armies went out on their conquests, they only took along sausages of horsemeat, and *koumis* (fermented horse milk) with a couple of horses. They slept on the saddles, and conquered half the world. We took a Boeing 737 and were only able to capture a few Uzbek playmates! What happened to the business ventures was history. Of course, it wasn't fair to blame everything on our side, as the inconsistent policies, and the consequence of vague ideological transformation that was practiced by the host country had contributed to the failure of the business ventures.

---

[29] MAS or Malaysian Airlines Systems is the national airline serving local and international destinations.

Chapter 19

My Old Volga

I have always had a great admiration for a particular old Russian car, a Volga model GAZ-M-21L, or famously known as GAZ 21. It was a strong car and was solid like a tank. Therefore, when I was told that someone would like to sell the car, I quickly went to meet the owner, an old man of perhaps over 75 years of age. The car was named after one of the great rivers in Russia. The "banana-leaf' green coloured car was in a very good condition, and was well-maintained by its owner. Actually, the old man was reluctant to sell the car, as he loved the machine so much. The car was presented to him by the Central Government (Moscow), when he was appointed as the member of Central Committee for Uzbekistan Communist Party. Obviously it had sentimental value for the former leader. I was told that he would polish the car everyday, but never drove it out of the compound for years now, as his eyesight was very poor. However, his sons managed to convince the old man to let go of the car, as he couldn't drive it anymore, and he could use the money to renovate the house. Finally, he agreed to part with his beloved "lover" (the car).

It was hard for me to see tears rolling down the old man's cheek, as he was staring at the money in my hand for a long time. He seemed to be in a doubt on whether he had made the right decision or not. Afraid that he would change his mind, I handed the money to one of his sons and walked away, while whispering to my guys to come and collect the car later, as I couldn't face seeing the old man who was clearly depressed at that time

We had a great fun with the car. When we went out in the evening in a group of more than five, we would drive the old Volga, as it can accommodate 7-8 people easily. In one of the night outings, six of us headed for the latest hotspots in town. After we had enough fun looking at the antics of Uzbek youngsters, we left the club for a late supper at my place. One of the guys didn't close the rear door properly, as they scrambled like a bunch of crazies inside the car. As I took a sharp turn in the city's main square, the improperly shut door swung open, and one of the guys was almost thrown out into the street. He was dangling while holding onto the opened door, and was frantically crying for help. Someone grabbed him by the belt, and pulled the guy inside the car. We laughed all the way home because of the incident, and we would talk about it over and over again whenever we got together.

There was another occasion when we decided to go on a hunting trip about 150 km from Tashkent. With our driver Mahmud at the steering wheel, the seven of us squeezed inside the Volga. We had another Uzbek friend who drove a new Daewoo Sedan with only three passengers. Still, everybody wanted to sit in the old car. Mahmud, known for his reckless driving, has been speeding at 130 km per hour throughout the journey. It was too late to realize what happened, as the car got overheated, and broke down in the middle of the highway in the chilly night. Apparently, the driver forgot to unscrew a valve to allow full circulation of water in the radiator. There was a valve in the radiator of Volga GAZ 21, which could be closed or opened. During the cold winter, the valve would be closed to limit the water circulation, thus keeping the engine warm. In the summer, or when the car was taken on a long journey, the valve would be opened to allow full circulation to avoid over-heating, and this joker Mahmud had just failed to do that.

We had no other choice but to send back Mahmud, and Ubaidulla the bodyguard to Tashkent that was 80 kilometres away, in order to bring another car. There was hardly any car passing by the lonely highway. If there was any, none of them would stop in the middle of nowhere to give strangers a lift. Mahmud and Ubai walked for miles, until they arrived at the Police Traffic Post. The Officers stopped a truck and asked the driver to give them a lift. The truck driver dropped Mahmud and Ubai near Tashkent's suburb. They had to walk again for another 6 km or so to my house to fetch other car.

Meanwhile, we were left freezing, as the night was getting colder. We made a bonfire, and grilled some "syashlik" that we brought along. Later that night, we ran out of woods for the bonfire, and we were shivering like crazy. We huddled together in the back seat, but that couldn't shield us from extreme cold. I was really astonished to see our new staff Naidu, who seemed to be unaffected by the cold, sat outside the car and puffed cigarettes, while we were freezing to the bones. Our Uzbek friend Vakhid was grumbling at my decision to take the old car for the trip.

Mahmud and Ubai then returned to us, after 5 hours of waiting in agony. We left the Volga at the roadside, and continued our journey to the hunting site. It was indeed a bad day, as when we arrived at the hunting site at dawn, the new car that we brought was stuck in the mud. We pushed and dugged the ground with our bare hands for two hours, before we could get the car out of the mud. When the sun rose, we realized that if we had steered away for about one meter, the car would have avoided the soft ground. Apparently, in the darkness of the night, we came too close to the lake.

As we were digging the car out of the mud, another friend Kuzavoi shot a wild duck. That was the only game that we got, after spending the whole night enduring extremely terrible cold and destroyed a very cool car.

On the way back, we arranged for the Volga to be towed back to Tashkent. The whole engine was damaged, and I had to send my loyal helper Amin to some of the Bazaars every weekend and scout for parts to replace the damaged engine block. We finally managed to repair the Volga, and hit the road again.

Once, I went on a hunting trip close to the Uzbekistan-Tajikistan border. After lunch, I quickly rushed back to Tashkent to meet the arrival of our big boss from Kuala Lumpur. As I was worried that I would be late, I stepped on the gas pedal till it hit the floor. At one junction, a Police Traffic flagged me down, but I pretended that I didn't see him. As expected, he jumped into his *Zaparus*, another old model of Russian car as old as the Volga, and started to chase me. Contrary to Volga, which was built for top party officials, the *Zaparus* is the smallest Soviet made car that was meant for ordinary citizens.

My Russian friend in Moscow, Sergei, used to joke about the *Zaparus*. He said that having a *Zaparus* is just like having a pregnant school girl (daughter) in the family. When

I asked why, Sergei said that "They bring embarrassment to the family". As I was blinking my eyes and tried to figure out the connection, he told me that the car would always breaks down, with the family members ending up pushing the car aside; much to the amusement of passers-by who observed the family's misfortune.

As I was speeding at 130-140 km per hour, I left the poor Policeman in a cloud of dust trailing far behind me. I decided to amuse myself by slowing down to allow him to catch up, but as soon as he inched closer, I rammed the pedal again, and left him in the dust as he was honking and flashing the head lights. I guessed I really had made him very angry during the 20km chase. Suddenly, I realized there was a Police Traffic Post with a barricade ahead, where every car would have to stop for inspection. I sensed a bigger trouble if I continued, so I stopped at the roadside to wait for the Policeman who had pursued me to arrive. I remembered very well of his burning red, angry face, as I profusely sought for his forgiveness, and claimed that I hadn't realized that he was trailing because he wanted me to stop.

The Policeman grabbed my document, and turned away, when I told him to read at the back of the document. It said ". . . immunity under the Geneva Convention . . ." I told him that he would create an international scandal, if he confiscated my document. Upon hearing that, the Policeman stopped in his track and I again apologized profusely, and told him that my big boss was coming and I was rushing to pick him up at the airport. I took out 400 *Soms* (equivalent to USD 5.00 at the black market rate), and said that I would compensate for his petrol and for taking the trouble to chase me at long distances. His mood did not change, but he took the money, and handed back my document, followed by a stern warning. The amount was about 20% of his salary.

Anyway, he probably collected 50 times bigger amount than his official salary from errant drivers like me. I continued my race to Tashkent, only to find out that a bigger catastrophe was waiting for me.

I adored my Volga and when I had to leave the country, I presented the car as a gift to my loyal helper Amin. Again, parting with the car had caused me to shed tears like the previous owner, but this time it was due to happiness. It was in December 1997. I understand that Amin is still driving the car, which would already survived over 45 years of loyal service, since it was brought into this world.

Chapter 20

Inspectorate Visit

Datuk MHT was a powerful Deputy Secretary General of Foreign Ministry; a no-nonsense person when it came to official matters. He was a Super Scale "A" officer while holding the post of Deputy Secretary General III, when the Deputy Secretary General I and II were only Super Scale "B" officers. As the Head of Administration and Service Division, he would make inspectorate visits to newly-established missions, to conduct post-mortem on the effectiveness of the Embassy Staff, as well as to ensure that all procedures and guidelines were adhered to by the Embassy staff in executing their duties. Obviously the Embassy staff would be on full alert, upon hearing that the Deputy Secretary General was coming for the inspectorate visit. That year, it was our turn to receive his visit.

A day before the weekend, I had a short meeting with my staff, to ensure that all necessary arrangements were finalized for his visit. One of the most important things that we did was to reserve a VIP Room at the Airport, so that the visiting officials would not encounter any problem that could arise, due to the strenuous and rigorous inspection process upon their arrival. Shahrom was entrusted to check on the VIP Room reservation, while Nazri was to reconfirm the hotel bookings. I told my staff that I would be going for a hunting trip during the weekend, and that I would probably be back late, so they should therefore wait for the delegation at the airport. I would be arriving later to the hotel.

When the plane touched down, my guys entered the VIP room to receive our boss. They were puzzled, as the big boss and his accompanying Accountant did not show up. After an enquiry was made to the Airport staff, they were told that the guests' names were not listed. Shahrom and others panicked and started to look around nervously. Tashkent Airport at that time was in such a mess and placed under high security control. No one was allowed to enter the arrival area, unless you had a close relative working there as a Senior Officer in the Border Guard Services.

After about two hours of waiting, they finally saw the boss emerging from the common arrival hall. The look on his face, as narrated by Muzakir the bank officer[30], was indescribable. Muzakir told me that as soon as Shahrom rushed to pick up his briefcase, Datuk MHT shoved him away. The first words that came out from his mouth were enquiries about the earliest flight to Kuala Lumpur.

Puzzled or rather confused, Shahrom asked the visiting boss why he wanted to know about the earliest flight to KL.

"I'm sending you home, Yes! By the earliest flight!

---

[30]   In 1993, Maybank had established a Representative Officer in Tashkent, followed by the setting up of a Joint-Venture company with the National Bank of Uzbekistan.

The annoyed boss seemed to ignore the Embassy Staff. Instead, he talked to the Maybank officer[31], as he sat in another car heading for the hotel.

I rushed straight to the hotel, as I assumed my boss would have arrived at the hotel two hours earlier. I had been delayed about half an hour by the Traffic Police on the way back from the hunting trip.

When I arrived at the hotel car park, I met Muzakir, the bank staff who told me to quickly go to meet my boss. He said my boss was really furious. Muzakir's facial expression indicated that something wasn't right. Without waiting any further, I rushed to the lobby entrance and saw Datuk MHT was just about to take his luggage and suitcase from the trunk. I approached from behind him, and quietly reached for the luggage. Thinking it was Shahrom, he pushed the hand away, only to realize later that it was me.

"Ohh it's you!" he said, and allowed me to carry the luggage. I kept quiet all the way until I checked him in, led him to the room, and asked if he would like to have dinner catered to his room. When he said he didn't want to take dinner, I asked for his permission to leave, and told my boss to have a good rest. When I came to the lobby, I asked my boys of what had happened. They told me that the VIP Room clerk had made a mistake, and listed our boss's name on a different arrival. I told the guys to go home, and wait for tomorrow's execution. Shahrom, who could still afford a smirk on his face, said that he was going home to pack his belongings.

---

[31] Maybank is Malaysia's largest financial services group and the leading banking group in South East Asia.

Early in the morning, I sent a driver to fetch Datuk MHT and the accountant from the hotel. He looked grim, as he stepped out of the car. Shahrom and the other staff were there too to greet him.

"So, this is our office Datuk, and as you can see, it's just an ordinary flat," I overheard Shahrom was telling the boss.

"Habis, hang nak macam mana lagi?", the annoyed boss snapped back. (Literally translated "So, what more do you expect?")

From that moment, anything said by Shahrom would receive snide remarks from the irritated boss. Datuk MHT first inspected our office premises. When he entered Shahrom's room, his eyes caught a plate, which read

"I'm not deaf but I just ignore you".

Even that funny plate turned to be the ammunition for the boss to fire him;

"You see, that's typical of you, even back home in *Wisma*[32], I was told that you were the culprit who pasted stupid remarks on the white board".

When the boss entered the toilet, he noticed cigarette butts in the toilet bowl. He yelled at Shahrom to come and have a look;

"Look, you throw the cigarette butts in the toilet bowl. It would not go away when you flushed it, and you would have to flush two or three times. No wonder we end up with high water bills!"

---

[32] Wisma Putra is another name for the Malaysian Ministry of Foreign Affairs. The name Wisma Putra was given to the original Ministry of Foreign Affairs building in Jalan Wisma Putra, Kuala Lumpur back in 1966. The entire Ministry moved to Putrajaya on 17 September 2001.

Actually, it was Naidu the clerk who had the habit of throwing cigarette butts in the toilet bowl. The boss didn't know the fact that water was almost free in Uzbekistan. We only had to pay the annual fee for the services, based on the number of occupants in the house. Anyway, it was pointless to say anything about the matter now.

Datuk MHT really meant business, as he quickly sat in the meeting room to begin the inspection. As the acting Head of Mission, I welcomed the visiting Inspectorate Team, and apologized for what had happened the day before at the airport. I said I didn't want to pass the blame on any of my staff, and I would accept the whole responsibility for the slip-up. I said the incident had taught us to be more professional in the future. Indeed, we had made the arrangement for the VIP room booking. However, having dispatched the booking letter, we assumed that everything would be fine. If we had acted more professionally, we would have followed it up by calling the airport to recheck the booking status. After all, there were only a few flights to Tashkent. This incident reminded us to be thorough in carrying out our duties, because only by doing so that we could distinguish ourselves from the Uzbeks.

Apparently, myself criticism approach worked, as Datuk MHT who took over from there said that he didn't wish to add further, because I had already said what he intended to say. He told us that having to queue up at the Immigration Counter for two hours next to the stinking toilet was one thing, but when he came out from the arrival hall, a few private taxi operators had surrounded him, and some were holding his luggage, while the other was trying to grab the suitcase with USD 120,000 cash inside, that was meant for our operational expenditures. The taxi drivers were actually just trying to win over the customer, but their persistence had greatly frightened our boss.

Although we were saved from the firing squad, Datuk MHT didn't soften his attack on Shahrom. As he looked through the account book, he picked up the remarks by the Ministry's Finance Division.

"This one, which is marked in red, meant that you have made an unauthorized expenditure. Let's see . . . . purchase of parabola antenna for Head of Mission. Well, there were only two possibilities of why did you make this purchase without prior approval from HQ. It was either you are the type of person who couldn't care less about the procedures, or either your boss is such an impatient person. You should advise him to wait for the approval. If he is the kind of fierce species who couldn't wait, then you should have put a note here; the purchase was insisted by so and so . . . . Then you should ask your boss to sign. By doing that, then you can cover your ass! In this instance, I took it that *hang memang kaki pengampu*! (you really suck up to your boss!)"

Nevertheless, I could say that we almost had a perfect account, as the Inspectorate Team could not find any serious mistakes or breach of procedures. In the end, the boss mellowed down, as the Accountant praised us for our good practices and good bookkeeping. Perhaps, it saved Shahrom from an early departure home. We chatted and laughed about the whole episode for weeks after the departure of the Inspectorate Team.

After the job had been accomplished, we gathered at Datuk MHT's hotel room and played cards. All other Malaysians who worked in Tashkent came to his room. We exchanged jokes and had a great fun.

One evening, I invited him to my house for dinner. I served him grilled lambs marinated with spices, and lots of garlic, which I prepared myself. He remarked that our living condition was bad, as two of us sat on the veranda, eating half of the medium-size roasted lamb. The grilled lamb and the shabby house reminded him of Mali, where he had served before. I guessed he left Tashkent with a glimpse of fond memories.

Chapter 21

Uzbek Wedding

The arrival of spring is always cherished by the Uzbeks. In April, the gardens and farms are blooming with cherries, apricots and apples, followed by varieties of fruits and melons that would flood the local bazaars till the arrival of winter. This is the time when most of the weddings would take place. The first shrieking sound of a blown long trumpet (horn) known as *karnay* in local language would mark the beginning of the wedding season.

Uzbek weddings are an elaborate affair. Be ready for the time when you would be rudely awaken from your sleep at 3.00 o'clock in the morning by the husky voice of local singers, accompanied by loud live band performances by a group of musicians, while the celebrated chefs prepared the "pilaf' rice to be served to the guest. Traditional musical instruments such as *tor* (a guitar-like instrument with strings), *rubob* (that almost resembles like the Russian balalaika), traditional drum *nagora*, and modern musical instrument such as violin and accordion were used in these performance. Some of the songs were cheerful, and were generally high-pitched. However, some sounded so pitiful, with melancholic melody, of which has strong elements of suppressed feelings, obliterating the cloud of cheerfulness. As I was curious, I asked a local friend of what was the song all about. The guy then told me that there were mostly love songs, that were something like . . . . ;

"Oohh my princess . . . . why are you tormenting me . . . . I have crossed seven deserts and scaled dangerous mountains to look for you . . . . Now I'm in your garden and could smell your perfume . . . . but you are hiding from me . . . . They offer me wine to ease my suffering but why do I need wine when I am already intoxicated from your love . . . . jonommm"

It was 3.00 o'clock in the morning! Hmmm . . . . it reminded me of the great poet Omar Khayyam who once roamed this land. At first, the howling and the wailing in the wee hours of the morning really irritated us, but we adapted after that.

Pilaf was served from 5.00 am till 8.00 am, but that is just for starters, as the real feast would be served in the evening. The early morning meal was only for the men. I used to attend such heavy breakfast with other Malaysian friends who resided in Tashkent. Pilaf is delicious if one is not too concerned about the cholesterol level in one's blood. But, for those who preferred spicy food, they would find that something is missing in pilaf ingredient. However, a little improvement could be made to improve the 'taste'. Our friend, Zubir, Chief Representative of Maybank Office would stuff a pocketful of *cili padi*[33] (a kind of hot, small-sized green chilli that could make some people jump out of their seats at the first bite), every time he attended the invitation

---

[33] A very small and very hot chillies.

for the morning pilaf. It was normal of us to end up in tears and a runny nose after the meals.

Coming back to the weddings, in order to formalize their marriage, the bride and groom would register at the Marriage Registrar Office. For believers, they would attend a simple ritual at the mosque performed by the local Mullahs to solemnize their marriage, before visiting the registrar's office. It is a tradition for the couple to undergo photo sessions at various monuments and important landmarks around the city, and accompanied by the full entourage. Their social status could be measured from the limousines that they hired, and the size of their accompanying entourage, as well as the cars that they drive, and where the banquet would be held.

Rich families would normally hold banquets at hotels, while most people have the weddings at home. The neighbours of the bride's house would block both ends of the street, and a special stage for the main table would be constructed. A special area would be reserved for the orchestra, as well as for the dance. Dining tables for other guests would be laid in rows on the street.

Prior to the highlight of the evening, the sound of the long trumpet, to mark the arrival of the groom, could be heard a kilometre away. *The karnay* (long horn instrument) and the accompanying musicians would lead the procession, together with the family members and close friends of the groom's side. As their number is large, they would normally hire a bus. I witnessed a funny incident involving one of those groups once. As the bus they were travelling in, and was nearing closer to the bride's home, the *karnay* player moved closer to the driver, and began to blow his heart out with his six foot long instrument. Out of a sudden, a dog ran across the street, and forced the bus driver to swerve to the side. The driver could not control the vehicle, and the bus rammed to a huge oak tree, and caused the *karnay* player to be thrown forward, with the tilt of his instrument was still in his mouth. The poor man lost four front teeth, when the instrument hit the wind screen.

The highlight of the day was in the evening, when the bride and groom would be seated at the main table from 8.00 pm till 2.00 am, or until the last guest would left for home. The bride and groom would be dressed in traditional costumes like Khan and the Princess. As the accepted norm, the bride must sit quietly beside her groom at the main table, and pretended to be naive, with her head bowed low throughout the evening. Raising her head would be considered as impolite, and all Uzbek girls must undergo this torture once in their lifetime. I guess the bride must be wearing diapers throughout the whole thing, as she was made to sit in her place the whole night or for at least six hours.

There were lots of food and alcohol on the table. The Uzbeks are Muslims, but they blame, or perhaps, appreciate the Russians for introducing alcohol into their culture. Soon, the effect from the strong drinks would add much fun to the fiesta, as the men and women started to dance to the live music till the wee hours. It was free for all after all. Men can invite someone's wife or daughter for a dance. It is an exceptional to the normal tradition. For instance, as if you are invited to the house for dinner, the host would hide their wives and daughters in the kitchen. But here, you can openly invite their women for a dance at the wedding, and in public.

When they got tired from the dancing, or when they feel that the musicians should have a short break, they would have an interval for congratulatory speeches and toasts. These speeches seemed to be taking forever, as almost everyone would not be spared from taking a toast, especially when you are considered as the guest of honour. I really hate this, especially when I am not familiar with the married couple. Who am I to give an advice to the couple of whom I do not know? Nevertheless, the drunk crowd would never let you go until you say something.

Sometimes, I chose to recite some prayers for the well-being of the couple. The trick really worked. The moment they heard the verses of Arabic being uttered, everyone, sober or drunk, would then rush to their seats and the place would fall silent. The musicians too would lay down their instruments, and raised their hands to *amin*[34] the prayers. However, they would continue with the drinking session and the boogies, as soon as the last amin was uttered.

The majority of the Uzbeks are non-practicing Muslims. However, when they hear verses of the Quran being recited, or the Arabic words are uttered, they would treat it with great respect. Many do not know how to perform *solat*[35] and could not even read the Quran, but they start everything with a prayer. Visiting guests are expected to read some prayers for the well-being of the household, once he or she enters the host's home. If you can read the prayers in Arabic, you are considered a special person. If one can read Quran, he would be considered a Mullah36, with the ability to solve many problems.

---

[34] Muslims, as well as the Christians used to utter it after they said their prayers.

[35] *Solat* means prayers and is one of the five pillars of Islam, the five duties required of every practicing Muslim.

[36] *Mullah* is derived from the Arabic term *mawla*, which means "master or "the one in charge." In Malaysia, it is known as *Imam* or *Sheikh*.

I remember an incident that involved some students from the Al Arqam group37 who were sent to Uzbekistan by its eccentric leader. At first, the locals resented their presence, when they encountered a group of strange people with peculiar dresses; men with robes and pointed turbans, and women covered with black dress and veiled themselves like ninjas. Some elders began to scold and chased them out of the building, when the boys and girls were noisily moving furniture to their new apartment.

The young boys and girls were puzzled and had almost gave up, when their quick thinking leader, Haris, began to recite some verses from the Quran. Out of the sudden, all the angry men and women stopped their shouts, and sat on the floor, as to respect the recitations of the holy verses. They dispersed quietly, when Haris had finished his reading of the Quran. After that, *Mullah* Haris and his friends were viewed with great respect and were regularly invited to read prayers at special occasions around the blocks they lived in. Their social status was elevated to a higher level of the society. Ironically, the Uzbeks didn't understand a word of Arabic, and they perceived those who converse the language as learned men.

The Uzbeks marry at a very tender age, even at the turn of the new millennium. Most brides would be in their 17 or 18, while the grooms are between the same age to one or two years older than the bride. The Uzbeks ladies are still

---

37   Al-Arqam is a Malaysian-based Islamic religious sect, founded by Ashaari Muhamad. He had a dream that he would soon be transformed as Imam Mehdi to rule the world, and the Central Asia would serve as one of the strategic centres for his empire. Therefore, he dispatched a group of students to establish the base in Uzbekistan. The movement was banned by the Malaysian federal government on 21 October 1994.

holding fast to their tradition to keep their virginity before marriage. Should an Uzbek girl face critical situation during an intimate moment with her partner before the marriage, she would "turn around", rather than face her lover, in order to keep her 'jewel' intact. You know what I mean. However, it is a different story after the marriage. Many wives would be willing to have illicit affairs, if they are pretty sure that the husbands could not discover their rendezvous with other men.

I have attended many simple Uzbek weddings by folks with a humble background, as well as the elaborate wedding ceremonies of wealthy and influential people. I love to observe people in their happiest moments. It was also fun to watch people's behaviour when they are under the strong influence of alcohol, as they could do all sort of funny things. I have witnessed a man who tried to flirt with his neighbour's wife, while dancing in a half-conscious manner, while the woman's husband was too drunk to notice it. I was not spared either. On many occasions, local women who were greatly intoxicated of alcohol, made embarrassing advances to me. Perhaps I was to blame too as my imitation of Shah Rukh Khan[38]'s dancing moves was too hot for those ladies to handle. Indeed, I was good at the traditional Uzbek dance, with some influences of Bollywood, and made good use of it to charm the local girls.

I guess, the most memorable wedding that I attended was the one in Shimkent, a city near Uzbekistan-Kazakhstan border. I was invited as the guest of honour by a friend, a local Don who hosted a grand wedding for his son; his

---

[38] Shahrukh Khan, often credited as Shah Rukh Khan and informally referred as SRK, is a famous Indian film star in Bollywood.

prodigy who studied in Malaysia and married a girl from Sabah, East Malaysia. When I arrived in the city, I was met by Shavkat, the Don's cousin, who was also a senior official in a powerful government organisation in Shimkent. He was tasked to take care of me by Don's order. The man in his early 30's took me to his house, and introduced me to his family. They prepared a good bath (sauna) for me, and allowed me to have a good rest before the big evening.

We arrived at the mansion just before sunset, and I was warmly greeted by the host. He showed in his stable a collection of pure-breed horses, and other luxuries of the house. The party was great; wines and vodka flowed throughout the evening, and the crowd was getting noisier. Then, there was a big fuss, with a loud and angry exchange of words. As curious as I am, I approached the rowdy group of angry men. I saw a few men were trying to calm down Shavkat, who looked as enraged as an injured tiger.

The commotion ended, when the Don stepped-in, and whispered some words to Shavkat and other men who circled him. They were all his "soldiers"[39]. I saw Shavkat nodded his head; he was clearly not satisfied. The host then approached me, and suggested that I could take leave and spend the night at Shavkat's home.

It was easy for me to extract information from an intoxicated man. Soon, Shavkat revealed about the incident, and was not supposed to let me know about it, as he should have kept it as a secret. Apparently, reports were made about the move made by a rival group in the region; a fact that angered Shavkat. Perhaps, under influence of alcohol, the matter was blown out of proportion, and the hot headed

---

[39] Soldier in the text is referring to the hitman who is working for the local Mafia bosses.

Shavkat wanted to retaliate at that very moment. However, he was stopped by the Don . . .

". . . No! . . . Not tonight! Not during the wedding of my son! . . ." said the boss.

Shavkat wasn't satisfied. While telling me the incident, he kept unlatching the glove compartment of the 4WD that we travelled in, and grabbed a fully-loaded Magnum .44 Desert Eagle. He shook the gun violently as he was cursing, then threw it back into the compartment. When he did that for the third time, I grabbed the gun, and pretended to examine it, and slowly tucked it at my waist, and out of his reach. I was just trying to prevent any mishaps, (or to be the victim of a misfired weapon). I tried to change the subject, but Shavkat was filled with anger. He bragged, and told that he was not afraid to kill people, as his close friend, the Attorney General of Shimkent, had given him a very useful legal advice in regards to this matter.

"Shavkat, if you really have to shoot someone, don't do it in a restaurant, or at a crowded bazaar . . . . If it was done at a secluded place, I'll see to it . . . .", said the AG.

Perhaps, that extraordinary incident had made that particular evening as the most memorable wedding that I had ever attended in Central Asia.

Chapter 22

The Khorezm Singer

I had a few real close friends, and one of them was this 40 year old bachelor Kuzovoy Otajonov (Kuzi). It felt comfortable to be with him for various reasons, but I think it was more of the feeling of a genuine friendship. Kuzi was a famous recording artist, until the turning point when he threatened to sue the government's Radio and TV stations that aired his songs. At that time, he had recorded more than 500 songs, which were being aired daily on local radio and TV channels.

Being a famous singer, he was selected to join the national cultural troupe for numerous trips abroad. Then, suddenly, he stopped receiving invitations for overseas trips. After missing a series of overseas trips, Kuzi paid a visit to the Ministry of Culture, and demanded for an explanation on why he was excluded. The reply he received had really enraged the artist. Apparently, he was told that since he had never bought any gifts for the officials who selected him for the trips, like what was normally practiced by the rest, they decided to exclude him from future trips. On the same day, he wrote to all TV and radio stations to stop playing his songs. He refused to perform in any official functions and retired from his singing career. When he missed the music, he would play his *tor*[40] alone at home, while in some cases, made performances for special friends. When the Minister of Culture came to know about the protest, he sent some officials to persuade him to resume his singing career, but the dejected singer adamantly refused. What a waste of talent.

Actually, Kuzi was hailed from the famous Otajonov's family of artist. His father was also a national laureate of Uzbekistan, and his younger brother Ortiq Otajonov is also a recording artist and is still active till today.

Apparently, Kuzi was not happy on many occasions. He said that he used to perform in a packed hall of Alisher Novoi Cultural Palace, but at the end of the show, he would only receive ten percent of the ticket collections, while most of it went into the pockets of the Ministry's officials. For this reason, he has a deep resentment against corrupt practices.

Hanging his tor, Kuzi shifted his interest to hunting. Actually, that was how I met him. I followed him to many hunting expeditions across the country. We slept in the freezing cold of the desert, and suffered severe fatigue and hunger in many occasions, as we were unable to get a single game, after walking and stumbling all day long. However, there were times when we came across thousands of migrating wild ducks, transiting at secluded lakes deep in the steppe land. Then, we turned the place into a war zone, until the barrels of our guns were too hot for us to handle.

One day, I took along my two assistants for a hunting trip far into the Uzbek-Kazakhstan border. We didn't find a single game, after a whole day of canvassing the vast territory. We were starving. Then, we met a shepherd with

---

[40] A guitar-like instrument with strings resembles Persian musical instrument

a flock of sheep. I asked my assistants to negotiate with the shepherd to sell us a lamb to be slaughtered for meals. Kuzi suddenly protested fiercely, and suggested that we pack up and leave the place immediately. I tried to reason that we could move after we have a grilled lamb, but he was adamant that we should leave right away.

A couple of months later, during our conversation, Kuzi suddenly asked about my assistants. I told him that they were fine, and still working for me. He said that I shouldn't trust those guys. He recalled the incident, when he had strongly prevented me from buying the lamb at the time when we were starving. Apparently, he overheard the conversation between my two assistants with the shepherd, who agreed to sell the lamb for twenty dollars. My guys were planning to tell me that the price of the lamb was fifty. It was obvious that they would like to make some profit from the deals. That was the reason why Kuzi was so furious. Nevertheless I never mentioned this incident to my two assistants, and continue to hire them, only to find out later that one of them was indeed a real swindler.

Kuzi was being very protective against any of the locals who tried to take advantage of me. And he himself never took advantage of our friendship. Indeed, there were times when he borrowed money from me, but he would always remember to pay it back; knowing very well that I would never ask for the debts to be paid. It was one of my weaknesses. In Uzbekistan, there were about 15 people who borrowed money from me, but they never paid their debts. I estimated that there were the same number of debtors in Kazakhstan and Kyrgyz. That number didn't include those who had outrightly cheated me in business deals.

I had a neighbour, Siradjiddin, who visited me close to midnight, and told that he had just returned from

Sukhandaria; a remote town near the Afghan border. He said that people there were starving, and there was nothing for them to eat (it was an exaggeration of course), and he came to know of some farmers who desperately wanted to sell their sheep for a low price. He suggested that we made some profit, if we would bring the sheep to Tashkent. He added that what he needed was 5,000 dollars, and a period of two days to arrange for the animals to be transported to Tashkent. He told me excitedly that we could make 2,500 dollars easily from the trade. It was a big sum for a country with an average salary of 40 dollars monthly.

I told Siradjiddin that I would lend USD 5,000, and give him five days to return the money. I added that he could even take all of the profits for himself, but with a condition that he must repair the leakage in my sauna room (Siradjiddin was a part-time carpenter). Actually, I could hire any carpenter for fifty bucks to undertake the job, but I just wanted to know more about this guy, thus entrusted him to do the job. The guy attempted to kiss my hands, while I was handing the money to him. I managed to pull away my hands though. Then, we parted for the night.

After two days, Siradjiddin invited me to his house to see the flock of sheep that he had just brought from Sukhandaria. What I saw was about 200 frailed-looking animals in the compound, and suggested for him to quickly sell them off, so that the buyers could feed them properly, or slaughter them, and put them out of their misery. But Siradjiddin suggested that we should keep the sheep for another three months, because most of them were pregnant. He reasoned by saying that selling a doe plus a baby lamb could give higher profit returns. As we were talking, one of the sheep gave birth. I just agreed with the suggestion, despite feeling a sense of uneasiness with the whole matter, and left him to do his bidding.

I almost forgot about the sheep, as I had a hectic schedule and would do frequent travels between places. It was until one day, one of my helpers told me that Siradjiddin had sold the flock of sheep a week ago. I quickly sent people to him, and passed the message that I wanted to see him. When I asked him about the money, Siradjiddin cooked up a new story. There was a brick factory in the Tashkent suburb that was offered for sale, and he used all of the money to purchase the factory. I already knew that I would never see my money again. Every time that I met the "new owner" of the brick factory, I would tell him to bring back one piece of the brick for me as a souvenir. Of course I never saw that piece until I left Tashkent. Meanwhile, my helper had fixed the sauna. These were the kind of people Kuzi was trying to protect me from.

Kuzi had always talked about the negative side of the Uzbek people. When I enquired on why he would always condemn his own race, Kuzi quickly responded that he was a "Khorezmi". Khorezm is a present day Khiva in the Urgench Region, that is located in the fertile Fergana Valley. During the Silk Route era, Khorezm used to be a separate power entity, and it detached itself from the Mavrounahr Empire. When Emir Timur (Tamerlane) came to power, he invaded Khorezm and massacred the men. Therefore, some of the Khorezmi would still carry strong resentment against the Uzbeks to this date, and refused to be recognized as Uzbeks.

When he was in a good mood, Kuzi would play his *tor*, and sang beautiful Uzbek and Turkish songs wholeheartedly. Indeed, he had a wonderful voice that was filled of emotions. As he was a constant traveller, his apartment was broken into by thieves for numerous of times. The thieves carted away everything that they could sell; TV sets and VCD players, radio, and hunting rifles. It was peculiar that they didn't touch his favourite *tor* that was wrapped in an expensive leather cover, despite the fact that the instrument, and its case, would fetch a much higher price than the cooking pots that the thieves stole. There was a possibility that the thieves didn't have any liking for music. But the most plausible reason was that they had a great respect for the talented musician. Stealing his instrument would be an inhumane act. One would guess that the thieves could be his neighbours who lived next door, and would fully understand that by taking the tor away, it would simply deprive him of good music and songs.

Kuzi was a good cook; a position that he took very seriously. He would never allow anyone to be near or disturb his cooking. One day, we caught some fish from the Syr Darya River, which we later took to the camping site. As the day was still early, Kuzi suggested that we look for pheasants or wild ducks. Before leaving the camp, Kuzi told another friend, who decided to stay back, not to touch the fish, as he would return and prepare a special dish from it. We were delayed for several hours, and when we returned to the camp site, our friend had cleaned the fish and cut them, and waited for it to be cooked by our celebrated chef. Hell broke loose, as Kuzi was cursing the poor guy for spoiling the fish. In anger, he said that it should be cut in a different way. Kuzi was non-stop shouting for about an hour, and only ceased his attacks, when I told him that I was not going to eat the food if I hear another curse from him. I told him that I saw a big *setan* (or the devil) standing at his side, and was helping him to prepare the dish.

In another occasion, Kuzi invited me for lunch. When I arrived, he was cooking pilaf together with wild pheasant, in a thick metal cooking pot called *kazan* by the locals. Being such a meticulous person in his culinary preparation, he took such a long time to prepare the pilaf rice. He told me that a good pilaf needs a minimum of three hours to prepare. As I was starving, I sneaked into the kitchen, and lifted the cover of the *kazan* to check if the pilaf was ready. You can guess what happened next, when the master chef realized what I had done. He was yelling profusely, as if my three second act of lifting the cover of the cooking pot would spoil the pilaf. When the abuse continued for 10 minutes, I put on my jacket, and left. As I was walking away, I told the irritated chef that I would prefer to have my lunch at the nearby *Chaikhana* (the tea house). He was startled, and tried to comfort me. When the elevator reached the ground floor, I saw him puffing and choking for his breath. Apparently, he rushed down through the staircase from the fourth floor apartment to stop me. He literally dragged me back to his apartment. It was worth the wait, plus the sulking act, as the pilaf was simply outstanding.

One day, Kuzi told me that in ancient times, every aristocrat or top military officials used to have a personal assistant of whom the former can entrust his life, plus he would obediently follow the master everywhere he goes. I already knew about this from novels and short stories I read. To my surprise, Kuzi then offered himself to serve me, and follow me everywhere go. I had a good laugh, and told him that I was neither a noble person, nor a rich man who could afford such a luxury. Furthermore, to me, he was more of a buddy than a helper. But I told him that if one day I have an increase in fortune, I would like to invite him to stay with me, and sing and play the "tor" for me, cook the pilaf, and to follow me wherever I go.

The last time that I heard of him, through a visiting friend, was that Kuzi had gone to Turkey, and the hardship that he faced had forced him to return to his old profession. In order to earn a living, he became a guest artist in restaurants around Istanbul. I was told that my buddy, the Khorezm singer, has many fans in Istanbul. Good luck buddy, I really missed you!

Chapter 23

Talented Painters

One evening, as I was sitting on the veranda, while chatting with a few visiting businessmen from Kuala Lumpur, suddenly, there was someone ringing the door bell. When inspected, I saw three young boys, with few rolls of paintings in their hands They wanting to show some of their artworks to me, so I invited them into the house. Nortoy, Asyraf and Zafar were final year students at Uigur University in Tashkent. They majored in fine arts, under the tutorship of Mehmedov, the National Artist of Uzbekistan. Nortoy came from Kashkadaria, an impoverish region in the South-West of Tashkent, while Asyraf was born in the neighbouring Tajikistan, but migrated to Uzbekistan, in order to have a better life. The family of the last guy, a good-looking Zafar, was residing in Yangi Yul; a place about 100 km away from Tashkent.

Having examined their work, we realized that the boys have great talents, and they were a versatile lot. They produced various techniques, ranging from portrait painting, still life, surrealistic, impressionists, and abstract works. My visiting friends bought a few paintings from them. After that, the boys would constantly visit my house, to show off their latest works of arts. I asked Nortoy and Asyraf on what would they do when they graduate. Then I asked on how they would go about and sell their paintings in Kashkadaria or Tajikistan, when people were struggling to buy bread for their family. As for Zafar, he was lucky to live near the capital. He could send his paintings to some art galleries in the capital city. Apparently, that was the greatest concern by both Nortoy and Asyraf.

In 1994, I bought a small flat, and converted the place into a residential place and a painting workshop, for both Nortoy and Asyraf. At the same time, I was helping them to promote their paintings among the expatriates. They sold many paintings to Malaysians working in Tashkent, and received many jobs to draw portraits for the Malaysians. Then, I organized their very first exhibition at Yow Chuan Plaza in Kuala Lumpur, which turned up quite a successful event at the time, as the economy was good at that time. The boys made some money, and managed to buy flats for their families. The boys had produced some great portraits for the family of the late Tuanku Jaafar of Negeri Sembilan, and the portraits of the Terengganu Ruler, His Majesty Tuanku Mizan.

One of my selling points when promoting these guys was that they can paint the portrait, complete with the character of the person. It happened that during the exhibition, they were assisted by Ms J, a lady with a strong personality, whom they would frequently engage in numerous arguments. Ms J requested that the boys paint her portrait. The guys had captured her features effectively on canvas, but the lady wasn't happy, despite the fact that those who knew her had testified that the portrait was indeed lifelike, and as perfect as a reflection in a mirror.

The young painters became close friends of mine, and they used to follow me on fishing and hunting trips. In one of such occasions, their presence had saved me from an awkward situation. It was a local holiday, and I decided to take Nortoy and Zafar to a place close to the Tajikistan border. The place, that is located at the bank of Syr Darya, was gazetted as a game reserve zone. There was a huge natural lake that became a transit point for thousands of flying birds, including wild geese, for their annual migration. The place is also a habitat for pheasants and wild pigeons.

The territory was closed for public, except during the few months of the hunting season. Travelling there at any time of the year was not a problem for me, as Mokhtar, the warden of the hunting zone, was a friend of mine. The warden, in his early 30's, lived there with only his wife. They had two sons. The eldest was staying with his grandparents in Tashkent, as there was no school nearby the hunting zone. The other son, a 4-year-old boy who used to run around and shoot me with his home-made arrows, has met a tragic death by drowning in Syr Darya.

When we arrived, we met a few other "privileged" men, who were allowed to come to the hunting zone at any time of the year. I guessed that they must be local officials, or perhaps those who served certain authorities. When we returned to our cabin in the evening, Mokhtar and his wife were busy setting up dinner tables. It was a national holiday; an event when everyone joined in the celebration. Perhaps that was why I saw a lot of vodka bottles were laid on the table.

We were invited to join the party. There were seven men and a woman crowding around a small table. Soon, fiery toasts were made as a dedication to the glory of

Uzbekistan, the friendship between the Uzbeks and the Malaysians, the well-being of the only woman in the group, and the ducks and pheasants that they killed that evening. The process would continue, if they found another subject to justify yet another round of merry vodka-drinking. Soon, they turned the secluded place, with lively shouting and singing. Someone staggered outside the house, and fired his rifle in the air, and screamed "salute!" The other fellow followed soon, and more blazing guns broke the silence of the night.

They continued on with the drinking and the singing, until late at night. When I saw that many guests, the host included, were already highly intoxicated and started to curse, I signalled to Nortoy and Zafar to leave for our cabin. Mokhtar, his wife, and others, were trying to prevent us from leaving, but they finally let us go, when I told them that we would return soon. We knew that after a while, they would be too drunk to realise that we were not coming back.

However, about 30 minutes later, Mokhtar's wife came into the cabin, and pretended to invite us back to the house. She sat on the bed where I was laying. The woman was so drunk and horny. I noticed that while I was at her home, she couldn't let me off her eyes, as I was trying to avoid any eye contact. She seemed to use every gestures and propositions that she know. The body language was clear; she was trying to seduce me. She then suggested for Nortoy and Zafar to return to her house, as she said that the guys were expecting them, and that both she and I would follow suit. I gestured to Zafar by shaking my head, and asked the lady if she could boil some tea for us. She later said that she would do anything for me, as she stood and made her way to the kitchen. I quickly whispered to Nortoy of a rescue plan. When she returned with the tea pot, Nortoy rose up, and told her that he would go and join the party. The woman's eyes were shinning with joy. As she stared at Zafar, he told her that he too will be joining the group after a cup of tea.

A couple of minutes later, Nortoy returned, and told her that her husband Mokhtar had sent him for her, as they ran out of pickles. She was visibly annoyed. As she was dragging her large bum towards the outside of my cabin, she whispered to me "You must come too my dear, or I would be very lonely without you there . . ." We froze for a few seconds, held our breath, and burst into roars of laughter, as soon as we figured out that she was about 20 meters away.

"She is like a leech right . . . . she would be sticking to you the whole night", said Zafar.

My relationship with the painters lasted till this day. Perhaps, they felt indebted to me, that they continued to follow me everywhere I go. When I was working in Kazakhstan, Nortoy came and stayed with me for months. I secured numerous portrait painting jobs for him that I got from among the diplomatic colleagues and rich locals. Then, together with Djambul, a famous Kazakh artist, Nortoy was invited to draw a large painting entitled *The History of Kazakhstan,* which was later placed at the Kazakhstan Cultural Palace in Almaty. They were only paid ten thousand dollars, while the actual invoice submitted to the government was much higher than that.

When the National Museum of Malaysia planned to organize an Islamic Arts Exhibition back in 1997, I loaned some of their finest works, together with my private collection of ancient, hand-written manuscripts and old jewelleries. Sadly, all of the items which I loaned to the Museum disappeared, when the Islamic Museum

Section was handed over to the Albukhary Foundation. [41] The Museum Official who received these items from me could only say sorry for the lost items, while the Albukhary Foundation declined to accept any responsibility for the loss.

Today, Nortoy is still active as a full-time artist, and he would occasionally visit me in Kuala Lumpur, while Asyraf is working as a "ganch" sculpture. Zafar was luckier, as he was employed as the arts consultant by Salim-aka, one of the two most prominent "businessmen" in the entire Uzbekistan. I am still helping Nortoy, Asyraf and another new friend Zair to sell their paintings in Malaysia.

---

[41] The Albukhary Foundation was established in 1996 by a famous Malaysian businessman Syed Mokhtar Albukhary; it owns the Museum of Islamic Arts near National Mosque in Kuala Lumpur.

Chapter 24

A Bazaar in Peshawar

Once, I took the Uzbekistan Airways from Tashkent to Kuala Lumpur via Karachi, while I was on duty as a diplomatic courier. It was fine on the way home, as the Airlines provided accommodation and meals at a budget hotel in Karachi between flights. Before leaving the Terminal building, the Airport Immigration Officer collected my passport, and placed it on the table. Fearing for the safety of my passport, I was reluctant to walk away, while the Officer was waving his hands "Go! Go!" I reminded him to not lose the passport. The irritated Officer opened a steel cabinet behind him, pulled out one of the drawers, grabbed my passport, and dropped it in the cabinet, while gesturing "Are you happy now?" I smiled, and left the counter feeling a little relieved. However, I tried hard to remember his face; the most striking feature of his was his handle-bar moustache.

Nothing much was there for me to see in Karachi. I walked around the shop lots and a bazaar. The city was deserted, as many people were still celebrating *Qurban Eid*[42]

---

[42]   In Malaysia *Quran Eid* is also referred to as *Hari Raya Korban* or *Aidil Adha* which means the Sacrifice Celebration

the day before. Pools of blood of sacrificed animals could be found everywhere; in bazaars and in front of the shop lots. I bought some mango fruits, and recalled the tragic death of President Zia-ul-Haq in the aircraft catastrophe, which was believed to be caused by a hidden bomb in wooden cases full of mangoes. The US Ambassador was one of the casualties in the tragedy. I really admired Zia-ul-Haq, for he had managed to fully control the Pakistani people from different factions, thus bringing the country to be a more stable nation. Before boarding that fateful flight, Zia ul Haq was seen performing a short prayer on the tarmac.

In the following morning, I left the Karachi budget hotel for the airport, to catch the next flight to Kuala Lumpur. When I arrived at the Immigration counter, I was a little bit alarmed when I couldn't find the handle-bar moustache officer. However, everything was normal when the officer who was on duty that day managed to locate my passport in the steel cabinet drawer.

On my return trip to Tashkent via Karachi, I encountered a problem at the Pakistan airport. The scheduled flight was cancelled due to technical problems, as explained by the Uzbekistan Airways Representative. I didn't buy his excuse. There were only a couple of passengers who appeared at the checking counter. I assumed that the flight was probably cancelled, as they could only sell a few tickets. At that time, Uzbekistan Airways was already in serious trouble, as they have huge amount of debts to Lufthansa Airlines, in the form of outstanding fees for the management of Tashkent Airport, and for the leasing of aircrafts from the German company. Once, Lufthansa officials "confiscated"

Day. It is one of the festivals that Muslims celebrate apart from *Hari Raya Aidilfitri.*

an Uzbekistan aircraft at one of the airports in London. It caused severe embarrassment to President Karimov, that he later sacked his favourite General Manager of the Uzbekistan Airways.

The Airlines Representative told me that the next flight would be available in three days time. I was begging and pleading for his help to do something, such as to transfer me on board of a PIA flight to Tashkent. He could have done that, but it would cause him unnecessary trouble. So, he ignored my plea.

When I could sense that there was no hope in getting his attention, I tried another method. With a raised and stern voice, I told the Airlines Representative that he would be answerable to any consequences, if I failed to turn up for the meeting with the President's Advisor the following day. I scribbled his name in my Diary as I was saying just that. I added by saying that President Karimov would be visiting Malaysia soon, and I was supposed to finalize some arrangements with his Advisor.

He took my bluff so seriously that he frowned. Just to add more dramatic impact and pressure on him, I took out a Diplomatic pouch from my suitcase, and shoved it into his face,

"Inside this diplomatic bag, there is a very important message from my Prime Minister to your President that I must deliver tomorrow. Now, you take it and send this bag to the Foreign Ministry. I don't care anymore!"

It was rather hard for me to control my composure (I felt like laughing at that time) as I noticed that his face turned blue. Serious, how could I even possibly leave the diplomatic bag to an unauthorized person in any circumstances? Honestly, I was so afraid that he would grab the bag, placed it under the counter and told me;

"Fine, I will take care of the bag and the documents. You can go now wherever you like . . ."

I would have peed in my pants if he did that. Anyway, to become a Country Representative for the Uzbekistan Airways, one doesn't need to be smart, but one would certainly need to be well connected.

"Give me a moment please!", he said as he was frantically making phone calls, and was rushing into several offices inside the terminal building.

I told to myself, and said that it was the only way to deal with these kind of people. Before that, he had demonstrated a 'couldn't-care-less' attitude, and discarded everything that I told him, like about all the troubles that I had to face due to the flight cancellation.

Ten minutes later, he returned with a radiant face, and told me that I was a very lucky person. He said that there would be a cargo flight that was about to take off to Tashkent in two hours' time. He had spoken to the Pilot, and they later agreed to take me in. I gave him a ceremonial Uzbek hug, patted his shoulders, and commended him for his great effort. I told him that I would be having a meeting with Ruzmetov, the powerful General Manager of Uzbekistan Airways. I also added that I shall inform the GM, and say that the Airlines Representative in Karachi is a very hardworking and helpful person. The Representative then personally helped me to carry my heavy luggage full of curry powder and other spices that I brought from home, to the cargo flight.

I was very certain that I would be taking a big risk, as I would not be covered by insurance policy. I was neither registered as a passenger, nor as a crew member, while I was on board of the cargo flight. Anyway, it was better than being stranded in Karachi for three days.

There were only six of us in that TU 154 cargo plane; the Pilot, the Co-Pilot, two technical crews, a stewardess, and me. Actually, it was far more comfortable than the passenger aircraft of the same airline. The cargo occupied the rear portion of the aircraft, and we had all the empty seats in the front section. As I was the only passenger, the Pilot gave me the privilege to enter the cockpit. It was interesting indeed to watch them manoeuvre the aircraft. As the open sky was clear, I could see a landscape of beautiful mountains from below.

The aircraft made a stopover in Peshawar, an isolated town located at the Eastern Afghanistan border, to load and unload some cargo. The pilot told me that the wait would be for about one hour. I asked if I could leave the airport to have a look around. He advised me to approach the matter to the Pakistani Officials there, while reminding me not to venture far if I was allowed to go out. He told me that they would take off without me, if I failed to return in one hour.

"If you don't come back, we would assume that you have been shot by the Talibans", teased one of the crew members. It was an effective scare tactic.

The Airport was deserted, as only a few planes landed at the airport daily. However, during the peak period of the Afghan war between the Mujahideen vs Russian-backed Regime, Peshawar, with its strategic location, had become a logistics centre for the delivery of weapons and other supports to the Mujahideen groups. During the day, the Airport would handle cargoes filled with humanitarian aids such as foodstuff and clothes, while clandestine flights at night would deliver armaments and other supplies for the Mujahideen fighters. At that time, CIA field agents had been working together with Osama Ben Laden from the other side of the border.

As I entered the ragged terminal, I approached two Airport Officials who were chatting among themselves, and asked if I could go out of the terminal for a while. I surrendered my passport, and told them that they can keep it until I returned. The Officer just waved at me and continued talking to his friend. "A real cowboy town," I thought.

Outside the airport building, I approached a group of illegal taxi operators who were playing cards and talking loudly among themselves. When they realized my presence, everybody stopped talking and stared at me. I searched for a less scary-looking face among them, and made a stupid blunder when I took out a 20 US dollar note and waved at him, while gesturing for him to take me in his taxi. A small scuffle then broke out, when the group of men were suddenly fighting for the only available customer around. The less scary-looking man suddenly showed his true colour, when he caught my hand and dragged me to his car, while shoving and cursing other men. Yup, it was really a cowboy town.

Once inside the old car, I told him;

"Airport-Bazaar-Airport. No Time", while pointing my watch at him.

Having said "ok", the man sped his taxi out of the airport. The remnants of the long war, that was fought at the other side of the border, can be seen and felt as we drove along the deserted road.

"Is it far . . . the Bazaar?", I queried, after braving for about 15 minutes of his crazy driving.

"No Sirrr . . . very nearrr!" the taxi man responded with a thick accent.

Shortly, I could see rows of flat-roofed, single storey blocks. Old men in Pathan costumes were selling melons, grains, spices and dried fruits. The wrinkles on their faces and jaded expressions revealed a story of untold deep sufferings. I really took a pity on them. Many of them were Afghan refugees; old men who escaped from the war at home. Very few women were seen walking the street, and those who I did see were wearing chadors (veils). I asked if we were already in the town centre, which the taxi man later replied,

"No Sirrr, the centre is very big, quite farrr from herrr. If you have time, I can take you therrr"

The taxi man took me to the back lane of one of the blocks. "Bazaar!" he said, while pointing to a place with some men, who seemed to be trading for something. It didn't take me long to realize the real nature of the 'trades', as I slowly approached the place. "Yes . . . this is real", I whispered to myself. There were Kalashnikov rifles, American M16, mortars, grenade launchers, old carbines, pistols, revolvers, plus anything else to cater to your heart's desires, except for the famous "stinger" (a shoulder-launched, heat-seeking missile that was truly feared by the Russian pilots) that was missing from the bunch. I guessed one could get it, if one asked for it. The armaments were laid in rows, and the prices were incredibly cheap!

Soon, I became the centre of attraction; something that I had tried to avoid since the beginning of the arrival. The traders surrounded me at the same time, with each and every one of them tried to attract my attention. A few even hold my hands to show their products. A man shoved AK47 into my arms . . . . ,

"Very good Sir. Only 100 US dollar, take it!"

I examined the rifle and then handed back to him, but he refused to accept the gun.

"Ok . . . 50 US dollar last price, very cheap Sir".

I wished I could buy ten AK47s. Other traders were also pestering me to buy from them. It was a very noisy market.

"No! No! Nahe . . . Men Malayzia dan . . . Ya ne smogu . . . ," I said, as I tried to use all of the languages that I could remember to tell them that I can't take the guns with me.

"Oo khojhent . . . Malayzia dan khe khojhen . . . . Nah biring . . ." (Hello Master . . . you are from Malaysia I see, take this . . .)

One man, who was speaking to me in Uzbek, stepped forward, and produced a Russian-made pistol of the Makarov model; a weapon favoured by the KGB bodyguards for its performance, good size and would give hardly any problem to the user. The Uzbek said that the rifle would be difficult to smuggle, but with the small pistol, I could just hide it in my pocket or in my underwear, while demonstrated on how to smuggle it to me. I thought that perhaps he is one of Rashed Dostum's men; the notorious Uzbek General who controlled part of Jalalabad region in Afghanistan. The Uzbek General once ran over a man with a tank, to instill fear among his opponents.

"Youq . . . Bathir . . . . Aeroport Toshkent Havo Yulari . . . Karimov Phewww!", I said, while pointing an index finger to my head. I told him that the moment I would arrive at Tashkent airport, President Karimov would put a bullet in my head.

They broke into a roaring laughter at my gesture.

I quickly left the "Bazaar" with the taxi man who had faithfully followed me around, and managed to go to a nearby fruit stall and bought some peaches. Then, we returned to the airport. Although I never expected for the taxi man to take me to that kind of "bazaar", I was nevertheless pleased and thrilled to be there, and experienced a real-life cowboy town. I only spent about 15 minutes in Peshawar, but the place had left me with such a strong impression.

When I arrived at the Terminal, the officer who let me out was still there. As I was in a good spirit, I took out a 10 US dollar note, slipped it in his pocket, and walked away briskly towards the aircraft. When I turned to look back, the Pakistani Officer was still puzzled why I had given him the money. I was hoping that he wasn't thinking that I had done something wrong and tried to bribe him.

Once in Bishkek, I was stopped by a Traffic Police for speeding. Actually, I had a stomach ache, and I was rushing to get home as soon as possible (later would I tell you about the conditions of the public toilets in Central Asia). To avoid possible delays, I slipped 100 Kyrgz Som note into the fold of my driving license, and handed it to the Traffic Police. I thought the Policeman would let me go without much hassle, since the amount was three to four times bigger than the normal "unofficial" penalty for speeding.

Apparently, he became suspicious and started to conduct alcohol test on me. First, he had to make a test device from a piece of paper by folding it into a cone shape. When the device was made, he asked me to exhale into the test device, and then brought it close to his nose to inhale and determine whether if I had taken alcohol or not. When he couldn't trace any smell of alcohol or spirit, he began to thoroughly check my documents, and found that they were all in order. He walked to my car and popped his head inside, to check the possibility of me carrying illegal items. It was too much for me to take, and I couldn't take it any longer, as my growling bowels were already at their limits. I walked to the opposite side of the car, and slightly opened the front door. As I slightly turned my body and pointed my butt to the inside of the car, I quietly released a foul, accumulated gas from my stomach as much as possible into the car. As soon as the horrible gas began to take effect, he withdrew his head from the car, and handed back my document while screaming;

"What the hell have you eaten? Rotten food or what? Get the hell out of here!"

Served him right for making me suffer that day.

A naughty friend once played a nasty practical joke on a Policeman who stopped him for a breath check. The Policeman had conducted the test by inhaling my friend's breath that was collected in a plastic cup. When the Officer returned his documents and driving licence, my friend profusely apologized for forgetting to inform the Officer that he was suffering from acute tuberculosis. To make his story a convincing one, he mustered a nasty cough as he sped away, leaving the Policeman in horror.

By the way, when I reached the tarmac where the cargo aircraft was parked, the Uzbek crew members were waiting for me, and joked that they were just about to take off without me, as they thought I had crossed over to the other side to join the Mujahideens. We headed for Tashkent, and flew over Afghanistan, while overlooking the rugged mountains and desert lands. It was one of the most pleasant flights that I had experienced, while being in a good company of friendly crew members. I shared the peaches that I bought from the bazaar in Peshawar with them, while we told jokes about the "Dushmans" (Mujahideen), the Uzbeks, Jews, etc. Sometimes the jokes were rather filthy, that we would be reminded by the only lady in the aircraft of her presence.

Chapter 25

A Jigit without His Horse

Some men are crazy about fancy cars or fast motorcycles. Some would love expensive paintings, and I believe that most men admire pretty women. But what I am truly mad about are horses, to the extent that it felt like an obsession. There is nothing that excites me more, than watching a flock of horses running wild on the mountain slopes. Most of Central Asian people, the Uzbeks, the Kazakhs, and the Kyrgyz, are fine horsemen. Excellent riders were treated as warriors, and were called the "Jigit". I was called a "jigit" too, not because of my horsemanship skills, but rather as an attempt to elevate my status, as well as a sign of my love of horses.

Once, I was travelling by bus to a mountain resort in Chimgan, which was about 150 km away from Tashkent. I found that there were so many horses along the journey to the mountain. Indeed, the place was perfect to raise horses.

"Look! That must be a Kaberdain, and that one a Qarabaer; the famous Uzbek breed! You see! The red one is so beautiful . . . . look at his long neck!".

I was in a frenzy mood, and shouted all the way like a small kid. I must have irritated the person who sat next to me, because in the end, he remarked that he had never in his entire life seen someone who was so crazy about horses. The gentleman was Tan Sri Hamad Kama Piah, the current President & CEO of Permodalan Nasional Berhad[43]; a prominent government-link conglomerate.

When I travelled to the Jizzakh region, located in the midway between Tashkent and Samarkand, I made a visit to one of the post-Soviet collective farms to inspect some of the horses. The place was dirty and in a dilapidated state. It must be a nice stable during the Soviet era. Having examined a couple of stallions and mares, I ended up selecting a young 3-year-old, long-legged stallion of Qarabaer; a famed Uzbek breed. The Uzbeks told us that when Alexander the Great invaded the land, he had crossed-bred his Macedonian horses with local counterpart, thus producing the Qarabaer. It was not the best horse at the stable, but I chose it because it showed a special affection for me when I touched it, or 'him'. His melancholic large eyes were following me with great interest, as he nodded his head and stomp his legs, while making hissing and shrieking sounds. It felt as if the horse was begging me to take him out of that miserable place. Having paid the owner, I named the horse *Nostalgia*[44] for a certain reason.

I wanted to ride the horse all the way back to Tashkent, but the distance, as well as the scorching summer sun, would have melted my spirit down. Two days later, *Nostalgia* arrived in Tashkent. I was overjoyed, but there was a problem to keep the horse in a very small space called my

---

[43] Permodalan Nasional Berhad (PNB) is Malaysia's biggest fund management company, a Government-Link Company (GLC).

[44] *Nostalgia* in Malay carries the meaning of wistful or longing for something in the past. It is also similar to nostalgic.

yard. As there was nothing much for him to chew, *Nostalgia* would gnaw the bark out of a vine tree, and destroyed a few cherry trees in the garden. Furthermore, I could not ride him along the routes in the residential area. Finally, I decided to send the horse to the suburb and kept it at a friend's house. In the beginning, I never missed visiting *Nostalgia* in every weekend, but after a couple of months, my affection for the horse was no longer strong. There were other priorities and new passions. The weekly affair soon became a monthly visit. After about a year, the visits became a rare thing, but I never missed sending enough money for his maintenance needs.

One day, as I was strolling at the park in the city centre, I saw a horse that resembled *Nostalgia*, except it was rather thin and fragile-looking, led by a bridle, with a fat woman and a baby girl sitting on it. In order to confirm my curiosity, I visited the place where *Nostalgia* was kept, and discovered the truth; the horse was not there. At first, the man was trying to hide something from me, but when I pressed further and mentioned what I had seen in the city park, he admitted the truth.

Apparently, the caretaker has 'leased' *Nostalgia* for a joy ride in the city park. It was done without my knowledge. I was deeply annoyed, as I had paid more than enough money for the caretaker to look after the horse. It seemed that the guy must have taken half of *Nostalgia*'s feedstock expenses, by judging from his skinny condition. I arranged for the horse to be taken to another place, where they promised to take a good care of him. I visited the horse a couple of times after that, as I was busy with other commitments, plus the place was rather far from Tashkent.

Perhaps it was a fated coincidence that I gave his name *Nostalgia*. A year later, *Nostalgia* was slaughtered, when he felt very sick. They discovered that the horse was infected with ring worms, which later destroyed his liver. The Uzbeks made "kazhi" (local delicacy made of horse meat) out of the poor horse. I could not remember if I had cried when I heard the sad news, but I certainly missed him very much, and regretted that I didn't spend much time with him.

When I moved to Kazakhstan, I took another horse from Akayev's (the ousted Kyrgyz President) stable in Cholpon Ata, near Issy-Kul Lake. It was a crossbreed of a Donsky Stallion, and an Arabian mare. I named the stallion *Satria*, that means "Warrior" or "Knight". The name also reminded me of a particular Malaysian-made car, *Proton Satria*[45].

Satria was huge and strong. He has a great appetite, and a friend of mine remarked that the horse's daily ration could feed three other "normal" horses. *Satria* was a very energetic and playful horse. I used to give him a shower during summer, and every time I turn around to pick up something, he would bite my butt or shoved my shoulder. When I turned to him, he would show his poker face, and pretended that he has nothing to do with the biting. When I turned around again, he would once again shove my shoulder and turn away, as if he was innocent. When he bit my back for the third time, and acted innocent again, I picked up a broomstick and threaten to hit him. The playful horse bolted away, sprinted around the residence, and headed towards the gate at neck-breaking speed. The horse came to an abrupt stop, when he saw two policemen (or our security personnel) standing at the gate with opened arms. He turned around, galloping, jumping and kicking his hind

---

[45]   The Proton Satria is a hatchback produced by Malaysian Proton in 1995 and ended in 2005 when Satria Neo was introduced as a replacement for the first generation Satria.

legs high up in the air. My two little boys who were playing in the yard got startled, and ran inside the house, screaming; "The horse has gone crazy!"

Truly enough, *Satria* has an unstable mind, and an unpredictable character. It was a "broken" horse. Soon, I discovered his weirdness and shortcomings. No wonder those people were trying hard to convince me to take the horse, and offered a good discount when I bought the stallion.

I would ride *Satria* everyday when I came home from work, and in some cases, it'll be just for a trot in the apple orchard near my residence. But *Satria* loved to gallop; perhaps he has a lot of energy from consuming so much hay and mixed cereals. Then, I discovered that the 200 meter stretch was too short a distance for him. Sometimes, he would venture under the apple trees, running with his head hung low, as if to let me be hit by branches and dangling apples.

Therefore, I would take the horse for a ride on a dusty road across the street, which leads to the mountain. As soon as he saw an empty space in front of him, the horse would gallop as if he had lost his mind. I was a good rider back then, but even I had a difficult time controlling the beast. Once, while galloping at full speed, *Satria* suddenly halted, and sent me flying over his head in front of a small trunk of fallen tree. It puzzled me that this big horse couldn't (or perhaps, wouldn't) jump over the trunk, as even a small pony could have done it without any difficulty. At that point, I could not understand the Stallion's behaviour. Sometimes, he would throw me out of the saddle, as he made a sudden halt if there was a small pool of water in front of his path. I sensed that perhaps there was something wrong with the horse.

From that moment I was always careful when having a ride with him, and would use only a special Kazakh saddle that I could hold on to, in case of "an emergency stop". Sometimes, I would just grab his mane to stop me from falling. One day, with *Satria*, we rode to a nearby village to visit a friend there. On the way back, I took the same dusty road. When we arrived at a junction, I steered the galloping horse to the right, but the animal kept running forward. Fearing that I would miss the junction, I pulled the bridle with all my might to the right, and yet he kept on running forward. Finally, I gathered all of my strengths, and tried to force the horse to turn right. My saddle slipped to the right side, as I had forced my weight on it. I then came tumbling down and rolled over several times on the ground.

Satria halted, and looked at me with his bulging eyes. When I recovered, I slowly crawled towards the horse, but the annoying animal then walked back a few steps away from me. I gathered my strength and stood up. As soon as he saw me standing on my feet, the horse galloped away, leaving me alone limping in the mountain. I then dragged myself home, and arrived when it was already dark. It took me two good hours to walk home. When I approached the residence, the Policemen who were on duty asked me what had happened, and told that they saw *Satria* running towards the orchard behind the house a couple of hours ago. Knowing what fine horsemen they were, I was too embarrassed to tell the Kazakh that I was thrown out of the saddle by a horse.

The next morning, I told my driver about the incident. In that very same day, he took the horse to the location where I fell yesterday. When he returned an hour later, he told me that the horse was "broken". But I could only see the bleeding of the right side of the animal's mouth. Janybek explained that the horse was only trained for equestrian sports during its younger days, and was used to the habit of running anti-clock wise. Therefore, he had no problem to turn left while speeding. However, it was hard for the horse to turn right, as he was not used to the routine. That revelation really explained the bloody mouth. If I was the rider, I would never have the courage to force the animal till it bleeds. Nevertheless, Janybek has indeed managed to make the horse turn right after that. As with the fear of obstacles on the ground, Janybek explained that the horse must have hurt itself many times during its jumping routines, thus developed a phobia so serious that it wouldn't even able to jump over a small tree trunk, or leap across a narrow drain.

Once, in summer, I led *Satria* to a hill not far from my house. When we reached the hilltop, I could see from a distance a flock of horses from a nearby farm down below the horizon. *Satria* made some noisy snores, but I didn't anticipate anything extraordinary in his behaviour, and I continued to enjoy the panoramic view from the hill top. Suddenly, he bolted, and jumped as how a bull would do in a rodeo, with a clear intention to shake me off the saddle. When I fell, the horse gave a short glance, and rushed down the mountain. By that time, I already knew of his intentions. I walked home, picked up my wallet, and headed for the farm.

When I arrived there, the farm workers had already reined the horse in one of the stables. *Satria* was bleeding in few places. I was told that he came out of nowhere like a lightning strike, and headed straight towards some mares. However, before *Satria* could demonstrate his prowess, he was surrounded by other stallions in the flock, followed by a fierce fight among the mares.

It is a fact that during spring, any of the stallions that wanted to become the dominant leader of the flock needs to fight each other to gain this position. Once the clear winner was established, only the dominant leader would enjoy all the harems, and the other stallions would abide by this tradition. Therefore, when an outsider like *Satria* tried to intrude the flock, a fierce battle would ensue. I paid the man for his troubles.

My driver advised me to sell *Satria* and get a better horse. However, I believed that I could still tolerate his antics, until one very fateful day, when I was almost killed by him. That day, like any other day, I would come home from work, and take the horse for an evening walk. That day, I decided to mount him without the saddle, as I thought I would not venture far, as I would be attending a reception later in the evening. I rode the horse through an orchard. After about half an hour, the horse became restless, turned around, and walked towards home. I pulled the rein, and urged him towards the other direction. However, after a few steps, the horse headed for home again. I lost my patience and stroked his thigh with a small branch. The horse bolted, and fled under the line of apple trees, as I lay flat on my belly and dodged the branches, as well as trying to avoid a nasty fall.

There was a narrow path between two abandoned buildings, where *Satria* and I would pass to enter the apple orchard. I sensed that something serious was about to happen when the horse didn't slow down, as he approached the narrow lane between the buildings. From the look of it, it seemed that if I let him had his way, I would have end up crushing my legs. So, in a split second, I jumped off his back and crashed to the ground, followed by a noisy sound of broken glasses. *Satria*, in his surprise, jolted and kicked his hind legs, with one of them landed on my head. I felt a warm blood gushing down all over my face. I took off my shirt to cover the wound, and walked to the house. The Police Guard looked at me with horror. I asked one of them to retrieve *Satria* and bring him home, and the other to call for an ambulance. After ten minutes of waiting, I instructed my driver to take me to the nearest hospital.

The doctor was preparing the stitches and about to shave my hair around the wound, when suddenly he asked how I ended up with the nasty cut. I told him what happened. To my shock, the doctor told me that if that was the case, then he must refer me to another hospital at the other end of the city. He said he would not take the responsibility if I happened to suffer any concussion or other injury. He recommended a specialist hospital to handle my case.

It took us two hours to manoeuvre through the rush hour traffic, before we finally arrived at the designated hospital. My wound had stopped bleeding, but I lost a lot of blood. After scanning, the doctors confirmed that my skull was intact, and I was a very lucky man, as the hoof struck on the hardest part of the skull. Later, a few happy-go-lucky young doctors pinned my head on a coffee table and started to dress the open wound on my skull, gave it six stitches, as they were noisily discussing about recent football match between Kazakhstan and Uzbekistan national teams. I was screaming in pain, as a pool of blood was covering part of my face.

"Oh, come on Jigit! This is not a wound from Chechen's bullet!", the Kazakh doctors teased me while roaring with laughter.

That's it. I was determined to make a special *kazhi* out of the crazy fat horse as I was recuperating in my bed. I then planned for the horse to be slaughtered and butchered at the coming weekend, with half for the *kazhi* dish, and the other half for *besh barmak* (a local dish made of boiled dough, and is eaten using "five fingers", or *besh barmak*).

Three days later, when the pain subsided, I ventured outside the house, and appeared at the door facing *Satria's* stable. As soon as the stallion saw my figure, he let out such a loud snore and shrieked, stomped his feet, and shook his head. I then approached the stable with a stern face. As I came closer, the animal's noise became louder. Suddenly, I seemed to be able to understand that he was talking to me, asked what has happened, and why didn't I take him for the evening walk for the past three days. His sparkling eyes were shining with joy. Alas, I couldn't even raise my finger at him, let alone running down a sharp knife through his throat.

Later, I was told that the horses which were trained from a very tender age, would easily develop a routine or a habit. In this case, I used to feed him an evening (meals) at 6.30 pm. It was precisely at the same time of the fateful evening, when *Satria* actually wanted to go home for his dinner. The horse became unruly, when he sensed that I had tried to deprive him of his evening meals.

A week later, one of the Police Guards revealed to me that his brother was a trainer for race horses. He proposed that I dispatched *Satria* to his brother's village, where the horse would be trained for a *baiga* (local horse race). I arranged for the horse to be sent to a village about 150km away from Almaty. Two weeks later, I visited the horse, and found out that it has lost a significant weight. When I enquired, the trainer told me that *Satria* was overweight, and in order to participate in the endurance race, the horse must shed at least 50 kilos. I was not an expert to argue on that.

After two months, I received the news that *Satria* has participated in a *baiga* at a nearby village, where he was trained. However, he never completed the race. What happened was *Satria*, filled with excitement, rushed forward from the starting point, and led the pack for the first three rounds. However, at the beginning of the fourth round, the horse suddenly stops running and walked away from the race track; much to the amusement of the spectators. No matter how hard the jockey boy was trying to get him back into the race, the horse just walked away, and started to graze in the nearby field.

On my way back from a hunting trip, I dropped by at the village to visit *Satria*. To my horror, I was shocked to see the pathetic condition that he was in. Once a fat and healthy horse, he was now somewhat like a walking skeleton, with an appearance as if the bones were about to burst out from his ribcage. I suspected that the Kazakh could have used the money that I sent every month to feed his family, instead of feeding my horse.

I bought 200 sheep, and kept them at a friend's farm in Baltabai, about 300km away from Almaty. After that, I took *Satria* to a farm, and handed the horse to the worker who was tending the sheep. I joked that he would be the only *chobon* (shepherd) in the entire country whose mount was a thoroughbred horse. Indeed, he has kept the horse in the compound at all times, fearing that it would be stolen. It was an epic story of *Satria*. From an elite President's stable near Issy-Kul Lake in Kyrgyz Mountain, where he was trained for equestrian, *Satria* graduated to become a shepherd horse, with the responsibility to look after a flock of sheep. Well, perhaps he was happy there.

I only visited Baltabai during the hunting season. The place is adjacent to one of the President's (Nazarbaev) exclusive hunting grounds. Due to the distance and the workload, I could only visit *Satria* for two or three times in a year. I was thrilled to see that he would scream and shriek every time he saw me coming. A year later, I moved to the Kyrgyz Republic, and then transferred to Moscow. Twelve years have passed, and my gut tells me that *Satria* was no longer roaming the Kazakh steppe. However, I never had the courage to ask my friend about his fate . . . .

Now that I have returned to my homeland, after many years of dwelling in Russia and Central Asia, my financial standing would never allow me the privilege of owing a horse. However, old habit dies hard. When I visited an International Agricultural Fair about two years ago (MAHA[46]), I stumbled upon a booth selling accessories for horse riding. Despite having acute cash flow problem, I bought a saddle, and kept it at my farm. Once in a while, I would take out the saddle from the store, wipe the dust clean, and keep it back nicely. As it for now, let it be known that I am just a Jigit without a horse!

---

[46] The MAHA Exposition biennial series is Malaysia's leading agricultural show. Hosted by Ministry of Agriculture and Agro-Based Industries, it certainly is amongst the largest and most comprehensive of its kind in the region, if not Asia.

Chapter 26

Hunting in Central Asia

There was a classic movie about the Russians' so-called 'hunting expedition'. It was produced by the Moscow Film Production (MOSFILM), and featured a famous Finnish actor in the leading role. The storyline was simple; a Finnish man, who reads a lot of literature about great hunting expeditions in Russia became so obsessed, that he decided to go to the country to have a first-hand experience. He was ceremoniously welcomed by a group of ardent hunters who took him deep into the Russian motherland.

As a tradition, at the beginning of a hunting expedition, the hunting parties assembled in a circle, and washed down their throats with a few crates of vodka the whole morning. By noon, everybody was too drunk to move around, and later dozed off for a couple of hours. When they woke up, the toasting resumed till the evening, and the whole bunch of unruly hunters was so intoxicated, that they lost all of their senses. This continued for days, with the hunters had yet to leave their base camp. The only time that any of the hunters ventured out of the camp, was when one of them went to get additional supplies in the form of a few crates of vodka.

In his drunkard slumber, the Finnish guy had dreams that he was in a hunting party with a Russian Tsar. Together, they rode a beautiful sledge while chasing after spotted dears; a scene that was coincidentally familiar with the one that he read from a novel. The following night, during a drinking spree, a few guys brought the guest to a nearby collective farm to visit some milkmaids. You know very well what happened next. There were many other hilarious incidents after that, but don't take my word for it. The best way is to watch the whole film entitled *The Great Russian Hunting Expedition.*

I guessed, the Russians must have brought this tradition forward to Central Asia, for I have gone through similar experiences during the 10 years' worth of hunting expeditions throughout the vast lands of Uzbekistan, Kazakhstan and Kyrgyz. In Uzbekistan I was lucky to have a rare, non-drinking Uzbek friend, Kuzovoi (or Kuzi). He also has a will so strong, that other hunters could not even force him to take a sip of an alcoholic drink. As an ardent hunter, he would immediately set out for a hunt, while others were raising toasts for good health, a successful hunting expedition, and world peace.

Hunting in Uzbekistan was mainly confined to small games, such as wild ducks, pheasants, with fishing included in the activity. Wild ducks and pheasants could be spotted in semi-arid lands along Syr Darya River. However, occasionally, some friends from the highlands of Chimgan would invite me to join them for big game hunting expedition on the Tian Shan mountain range. I only joined them once, as this kind of expedition would need a period of five to ten days away from the office. Anyway, during my trip with this group, we ran out of food supplies, and someone had to be dispatched down the mountain to get an additional stock. We waited three days for his return, and joked about whom should be the first person to be sacrificed for the survival of the group.

Later, after eight days of following some tracks made by a flock of mountain goats, but without the actual animals in sight, we decided to turn back and headed for home, empty-handed. Nevertheless, it was an achievement for some of us. In my case, I had shed three unneeded kilos off my weight.

During a certain period of the year, migratory birds of different species from Siberia would make a stopover at water holes in Uzbekistan, on their journey to warmer places. We used to set up camouflaged hideouts near the lakes or river banks. In one occasion, Kuzi and I shot down 247 birds of different species, and it took three days for us to clean them of their feathers. Kuzi would then store the birds in his huge freezer as food supply, and would-be gifts for friends. While most people make *plov* (pilaf rice) with lamb or beef, Kuzi would serve special *plov* cooked with pheasant or wild goose.

I had followed Kuzi to all corners of the vast Uzbek lands, and fulfilled a complete cycle of experiences that a seasoned hunter should endure. The readers would find more information about this good man in the earlier chapter entitled *The Khorezm Singer*.

When I was transferred from Uzbekistan to Kazakhstan, among the first things I did was to establish contacts with some locals who shared my passion of hunting. I wrote a private letter to President Nazarbaev to seek his permission to purchase a hunting rifle. My request was granted, much to the envy of the Pakistani Ambassador, who revealed that his request was denied, when he sought permission to buy an air rifle. Anyway, my firearm became my companion whenever I hunt through many steppe lands, as well as the venture through numerous mountains.

After awhile, my hunting adventures became known among the diplomatic community. I started to receive numerous requests for me to include them in my next hunting expedition. However, I was rather selective about sharing my private hobby. Therefore, only a selected few were admitted into my personal circle.

As a matter of fact, I viewed most of my diplomatic colleagues as a group of spent forces whom would not be able to withstand physical hardship; a quality that is needed for a hunting expedition. I thought that it was better for them to stay at home, and enjoy their finest wines, or invite friends for a game of poker or bridge. Otherwise, they could also accompany their spouses to bazaars, or visit newly-opened malls during weekend.

My good friend, Muhammad Beruni, the second person in charge of the Libyan Embassy, had been nagging me for a long time to be taken on a hunting trip. I tried to reason out, and joked that he was too old and unfit for such challenging adventures.

". . . . It's no fun you know. This trip would be very tiring, gruesome and dangerous. In the event of a catastrophe or serious mishap, I would not be able to carry you home . . . . you see, you are overweight . . . .", I kid.

"Well . . . . if such incident happen, you can just leave me to the wolves in the steppe . . . . only please take me with you alright . . . .", Beruni pleaded like a young kid. He knew I was exaggerating.

"Maybe you have a Kazakh girlfriend waiting for you there. That's why you didn't want to take me along. Don't worry, I promise I will not tell a word to your wife . . . ." It was his turn to pull my leg.

Finally, one day, I told him to get ready, as we would be going for a hunting trip to Baltabai in the coming weekend. I told Beruni that I also invited Marcello, a Cuban Ambassador, to join us. Beruni was please to hear that, as Ambassador Marcello was a fun company to be with. He was a jovial and funny person. At the age of 50, the slender, tall, dark and handsome man was the fittest among us. He was formally a sportsman and a boxer. Having graduated from Moscow State University, Marcello spoke fluent Russian. He married at the age of 40 to a stunning beauty, who was 20 years younger than him.

We had agreed to meet at the Main Square near the Presidential Cultural Palace in the city centre on the appointed day. Beruni was the first person to arrive. He was in a high spirit. Donning a fisherman hat and a khaki trousers, he looked funny to me, as I remarked that I expected him to be in stripe robes with woollen skullcap; an attire similar to the one donned by Kaddafi, when the latter addressed the crowds at his hometown in Surt.

Next came Ambassador Marcello, who was dropped off by his personal driver; his beautiful wife Eva Maria. Upon seeing me, the lady lowered the car window and said;

"H . . . . please take a good care of my man, okay . . . ."

"Are you kidding . . . . he is the fittest among us, don't you see . . . .", I retorted.

"I'm talking about not letting him stray to the left! That's what I meant, and remember to bring back pheasants with feathers fully-intact, so that I could differentiate them with chicken sold at bazaar . . .".

All of us broke into a hysterical laugh. Once inside the car, I said to Marcello that he must have been a naughty boy, as depicted through his wife's paranoia. Earlier, I had asked the Cuban Ambassador to take the front passenger seat.

"Please take the front seat and serve as our bodyguard. Your priority now is to protect this guy next to me, As Sheikh Muhammad Al Beruni, who would soon replace the Great Leader of the People of Libyan Jamahirriya . . . .".

We continued to make fun of each other, as we were travelling in a Nissan Safari 4WD, that was driven by Erzat, a local young man who had served in Afghanistan during Soviet-Afghan war. Erzat was captured by the Mujahedeen during one of the fierce battles. As the Afghans were lining him in front of the firing squad together with other captured Russians, Erzat had asked for a permission to perform the *solat*. The Mujahedeen allowed him to undertake the ritual under watchful eyes of their Commanders. Apparently, that quick thinking act had saved his life, as he was later freed by the Mujahedeen. However, the bullet wound that he suffered from the war has always given him a lot of problems. I always have a strong feeling to certain people during the first encounter. When Erzat came for the interview as a driver, I didn't ask questions such as his knowledge about the engine, or if he was familiar with roads around the city. However, I remembered asking him what he would do if I was suddenly clobbered by some drunkard Kazakhs who are six feet tall, and huge as a breeding bull. His answer must have pleased me that I ended up choosing him out of 40 odd guys who attended the interview.

I specifically bought that 4WD for this purpose. The car had taken me to all corners of Central Asia. The Diplomatic registration plate had saved me a lot of troubles during those many years in Uzbekistan, Kazakhstan and the Kyrgyz Republic.

We then headed for Almaty-Kashgar highway, a border city between Kazakhstan and China. The intended destination was Baltabai, about 300 km from Almaty.

There was vast steepe land covered in short grass. However, thick bushes and tall grass called *kamish* (similar to jut) were abundant around wet grounds or near the streams. The place was inhibited by birds like pheasants, ducks and quails, as well as a breeding ground for game animals such as deer, gazelles, wild boars and foxes. However, there was something else so dear and close to my heart in Baltabai; it was there where I kept *Satria*,my favourite Stallion. I was longing to see my lover.

I started a debriefing session on safety measures on the use of firearms, as soon as we hit the highway. Since Marcello was familiar with those issues, I directed my briefing at my old Libyan brother, Beruni. When I noticed that he didn't take my advice seriously, I suggested that I would give him a gun with blank cartridges.

"Oh come on H . . . . Don't worry, I'm not going to shoot at your butt . . . .", he said.

Then the conversation centred on the most pertinent issue.

"Listen here carefully brother Muhammad. I know Marcello can handle this very well, but for you, please remember this . . . . As soon as you sit at the table, our host would offer a toast . . . normally vodka is the medium. I know that you don't drink, therefore don't you ever accept the glass . . . . You can tell the Kazakhs that you never drink alcohol in your life, as you are descendent of the Prophet Muhammad . . . . or you can cook up a story by telling them that you would easily loose control, and became very violent if you consume alcohol. In my case, I told them that I am suffering from acute liver problem due to excessive intake of alcohol in the past, and now doctors told me that I shouldn't take alcohol at all if I want to live another year. Once you have started, there's no turning back for you brother . . . . ".

I proceed to inform Marcello and Beruni about how I came to know of our host, as well as stories of my previous trips. Then our conversation shifted to latest gossips about the diplomatic circle in Almaty. Suddenly, the name of Ambassador Ramazan was mentioned. Marcello and I started to laugh hysterically, to the bewilderment of Beruni. Ramazan was Beruni's boss. Prior to his arrival, Beruni headed the Libyan Embassy in Almaty as Charge d' Affaires. Ramazan was a political appointee, but not a career diplomat, compared to Beruni who had served for over 30 years in the Libyan Foreign Ministry. As a matter of fact, Beruni was more qualified and fit to be the Ambassador, instead of this young man; a man who used his connection as the leader of a youth movement back home to lobby Kaddafi for the post. Not many people were fond of Ramazan, perhaps due to unpolished character or lack of substance. Therefore, many Heads of Mission (HOM) still maintained good contact with Beruni, instead of befriending the new Ambassador.

A week before, the Kazakh government invited all HOM to Astana to attend an official function. Of late, the Kazakh President seemed to intensify his campaign to promote the Republic's new capital, Astana.[47] The only major setback was the refusal of foreign diplomatic missions to move their offices to the newly built capital in the middle of the steppe land, that was infested by fly-sized mosquitoes. I was merely exaggerating, of course. Sometimes, the Foreign Ministry

---

[47] From a provincial town with population around 200,000 situated in the middle of the steppe land, today, Astana has transformed into one of the modern cities of the world, as its residents have multiplied in numbers. All foreign diplomatic missions have moved to the new capital.

would arrange a chartered flight for us to attend functions in the new capital. In another time, we would be dispatched in a special wagon from Almaty to Astana, where we would spend a night on the train.

Anyway, while we were on the flight to Astana, Marcello and I noticed the peculiar behaviour of the Libyan Ambassador. We observed that Ramazan could not stay put in his seat during the flight. Five minutes after the plane took off, while the warning lights were still displaying, this man would rise from his seat, and began to walk along the isle back and forth, much to the annoyance of the cabin crew and some passengers.

I saw Marcello's eyes were shining, and I knew he was scheming up a plan or something. Then I saw the Cuban Ambassador moved to occupy one of the empty seats in the middle section of the aircraft that was near the cabin crew area. He was seen to discuss something to a stewardess in a very suspicious manner. When I saw two other cabin crews joined the discussion with Marcello and the stewardess, I stood, and move quietly to occupy an empty sit behind Marcello. I didn't want to be left out from whatever scheme that he was planning. I then heard that Marcello asked the stewardess if she has some sanitary pads.

". . . . Excuse me Your Excellency . . . . why do you need the pads?", queried the stewardess. Her facial expression was a mixture of seriousness and a funny face.

"Ohh . . . it's not for me, but for Ambassador Ramazan", quipped Marcello, while pointing at the Libyan Ambassador who was walking the isle back and forth.

". . . I'm sorry Sir, but why does he need the pads . . . ." the puzzled lady asked.

". . . *Prosti menya shto zabil skazat . . . U nevo strashno gimaroi . . . . i poetomy nuzhen prakladka . . . . bednie gaspodin . . . . On sam ne udobna poprasit I khodit tuda suda tuda suda kak medved v kletke . . . ."*

(Pardon me, for I forgot to tell you that he has serious problem with haemorrhoids, and therefore he needs sanitary pad, so that he could sit and not stain his trousers . . . . poor gentleman . . . he is too shy to ask . . . . What he could do is to walk back and forth like a bear in a cage).

The ladies whispered to each other, and one of them reached for her handbag, took out a few pieces of sanitary pads, and handed them to the leading stewardess. The lady approached Ambassador Ramazan, stood in front of him for a moment, while struggling to find some suitable words for him. The young Ambassador was seen posing a sweetest smile. The stewardess then whispered something to Ramazan's ears, as she shoved the pads into his hand. Clueless, Ramazan brought the pads before his eyes. In a matter of seconds, his flirting smile disappeared;

"What is this . . . . Is it a joke!

"Errr . . . . Your friend told me that you need this, but you were too shy to ask for it, so he had asked us to give it to you . . . ."

The irritated Ambassador hissed, walked away, and went straight for his seat. He slammed his big physique in his seat, and startled the sleeping gentleman who was sitting next to him. He didn't even apologize. By that time, Ramazan had already knew that someone was playing a practical joke on him.

Meanwhile, Marcello held his head down, with one hand holding his forehead. He was seen visibly shaken, as he tried hard to suppress his chuckle. I almost had a cramp in my stomach as I tried to regain my composure. I narrated the whole incident, much to the amusement of Beruni. He asked if Ramazan came to know who played the trick on him. I said that even if he knew, he wouldn't dare to challenge the former Middleweight Champion of Cuba. We both broke into laughter.

With all kinds of anecdotes and funny life stories, we hardly realized that two and a half's hours had passed, and we were already in Baltabai. Our host, an influential man who served as one of the Presidential advisors and few other people, were waiting for us. After quick greetings and introduction, I quickly headed to a stable not far from our host's home, as my colleagues were ushered into the house. Beruni was concerned about my absence, but the host assured him that I would be fine.

I was just about to open the gate when I heard a loud shriek from *Satria*. I ran towards the stallion, that was stomping his feet while shaking his head noisily.

"Jonom . . . you still remember me . . . . I'm so sorry, I couldn't come here as often as I wish . . . .".

I was talking to the horse, while warm tears started to roll down my cheeks. I caressed the stallion's head, and patted his body. *Satria* looked fine, although he was not as healthy as when he was under my care. I talked incessantly with the horse as if he understood all of my words, while I asked if he was happy there, whether the caretakers treated him well, and had he looked after my sheep. I wanted to spend a few more moment with *Satria*, but the presence of a boy had interrupted the session. They sent him off to tell me that they were ready to leave for the hunting ground.

I bid goodbye to *Satria*, and walked away with a heavy heart. *Satria* became unruly, and made a lot of noise when I left. The horse must have been broken-hearted as well, as if he understood that this would be one of the few last visits from me. Again, I was overtaken by the emotion, and warm tears began to flow again, with them dripping down my cheeks and chin. I quickly wiped out my tears away.

The host ushered me into the house, where my friends and few other locals were gathering around a large table full of foods and drinks. I sat quietly at one corner, while answering questions absent-mindedly. I guessed that they must have realized what was going in my mind at that time. The man who was entrusted to look after my horse was summoned into the room. He looked so frail and miserable. Since our arrival, he was busy making preparations for the hunting party, food provisions, vodka, guns and other hunting gear. During the old days, he would have been a slave, but in the modern time, he is called a helper. The job, social status and responsibilities were just the same, regardless of time.

The man of the house started to ask him about the condition of *Satria* and other matters related to the horse, as if I have not seen the horse for myself. The frail men accomplished his part as he was expected to do, and revealed to me that the horse was fine and healthy so on. When I found the opportunity to interrupt his story, I rose and suggested that we leave, because the weather was expected to be ghastly. Everybody agreed at my suggestion, and rose the glass to offer a toast for a successful hunting.

At the same time, my host's nephew, fully-dressed in the uniform of Kazakhstan Traffic Police (GAI), came to bid farewell, as he would be leaving for work. They wished him good luck in his "hunt" too. Everybody seemed to understand the connotation, and broke into small laughters. It was a great privilege to be a Traffic Policeman, and stationed at roadblocks at one of the busiest highways, like the Almaty-Kashgar highway. Every day, tens of thousand of heavy-loaded trucks with merchandises from China would passes by, and they have to stop at the checkpoint for an inspection. It could be a brief, less-than-a-minute at the documents, or it could be a whole day affair. In any case, everybody knew the standard 'rate' that people have to 'pay' in order to avoid the red-tapes.

We reached the hunting zone after about 20 minutes of ziz-zaging through the dirt road, while trying to avoid deep potholes. It was the befitting time to show off the prowess of my mount, the Nissan Safari 4WD. The vehicle would skid to the left and right, plunged into deep potholes, stuck in mud, and yet it came out solid and elegant. Local friends in the Soviet–made 4WDs, the Kamaz, and a much smaller Lada were doing just fine too.

We stopped on a flat ground, and came out of our vehicles with our raincoats, as the rain was getting heavier. There were vast steppe lands before our eyes. I turned to Beruni, who stood next to me, and whispered that if he felt that he could not take it, he could stay back in the car.

"Sir . . . please do not underestimate me. I used to go for pheasants hunting in Pyongyang . . . .", the veteran diplomat protested in thick Arabic accent.

"But it was 20 years ago . . . . perhaps you were 50 kg less heavier . . . .", I said, while still in the mood to tease him.

Guns and rifles were handed out to everybody. Our host brought a trunk load of fire powers. I had my very own semi-automatic rifle, with the capability to load 5 cartridges at once. It was a beautiful piece of 'toy'. However, the gun was rather heavy, as its barrel was slightly longer than other hunting rifles. Having witnessed that Beruni was undecided to choose his piece, I suggested that he took a double-barrel shotgun "BAIKAL". It was easy to handle, as the gun has one trigger, while most of other double-barrel shotguns have two triggers. Sometimes, under demanding situations, one would get confused and pulled the trigger on an already empty barrel, causing him to lose a couple of good seconds, which made a lot of different in certain circumstances. In two split seconds, while you were struggling to find out which is the right trigger, wild ducks would dash over your head at 120 km/hour. When you raised your head the second time, all you could see were glitters of their colourful tails vanishing into the distance. As for Marcello, he grabbed an AK47. After I had told him that we were going for pheasant shooting, he changed it with a shotgun. However, he ended up taking both the AK47 and the shotgun, when someone said that we might bumped into deer or gazelles.

Another toast was raised before the march. Beruni, who managed to skip the ceremony, was grinning at Marcello and said";

"Tell me honestly Marcello . . . . Are you alright . . . . If you are drunk, then I don't want to walk with you . . . .".

The Cuban Ambassador just laughed away. There were eight of us in the hunting party. We made a straight line, standing about twenty meters from each other, and began to march forward. I stood at the end of the line on the far left side. It was the beginning of autumn. The cold rain and strong wind had caused the temperature to drop significantly. I started to freeze and had a runny nose. I guessed that Beruni must have experienced the same thing. However, other guys were not affected by the cold weather. It was the Vodka that helped them to overcome the chilly morning. I later thought briefly, and contemplated that only some crazy bunch of men would go out under such weather condition.

We walked on soft muddy ground. After ten paces, the soles of our long boots were stuck with clay, with each weighing about two kilos on each shoe. Besides unnecessary weight, it was very uncomfortable to drag your feet in thickets of bushes under this circumstance. The boots that were given to me was two sizes bigger, and would always come off when I lifted my foot due to the excessive weight. I was frustrated and became undecided on whether I would continue my journey or not.

Suddenly, after about 10 minutes walk, we were stunned by sudden shrieking sound of a startled male pheasant, while the beautiful cock rose from a thicket, and flew away. The two guys who were the closest to the bird fired, and one of them brought down our first trophy. My spirit was elevated. Soon after that, we came across a few more birds. The hunt became merrier. I was yet to fire a shot, as those birds were flying towards other directions from where I stood. I saw Beruni fired a couple of shots, but I wasn't sure if he hit anything.

Someone managed to hit a big pheasant, and the bird fell. However, the big bird ran away, as it hit the ground. The guy fired again at the bird, which later made a pass at my position. I was fortunate to see what was happening. In a split second, I dived flat to the ground, as the spray of cartridges hissed over me. I yelled;

"Ostorozhno . . . . khachu zhit esho ne mnozhko liet . . . .".

(Careful . . . . I want to live a couple more years . . .).

I heard some commotions from the other side of the bushes, and words of apologies and precautions were uttered. My current location and other hunters were separated by some bushes and tall grass *kamish*, which grew along a small stream. Startled game animals, pheasants and quails would dash into those thickets to hide from hunters.

Suddenly, a gazelle sprang out from some bushes about ten meters from me, and leaped towards my colleagues. I was caught by surprise, and could only raise my gun, but was unable to take a shot at the animal. Gazelles have a peculiar style of making a run, as they bounced up in the air as if their legs were made of springs. In two leaps, the gazelle was already out of my sight. At that point, shots were fired from multiple directions. It was like a war zone. Again, I dived to the ground and lay flat until it was all over. It was a bad omen. Within five minutes, I barely escaped possible injury or death. The third time could be fatal, so I decided to turn back. After all, it was very uncomfortable to continue under such circumstances. I was freezing, while having a runny nose, as my body was soaking all over from endless rain, and was struggling with my heavy boots that were thick with mud.

I slowly walked back to the place where we left our vehicles, and realized that my driver had taken the key with him. For the next five hours, I took cover from the rain and cold wind at the side of the 4WD. I was freezing and hungry.

I later snoozed off, and was awakened by a commotion by the hunters that were slowly returning to the base. In a distance, I could see Beruni in such a terrible situation. He could hardly drag his feet, as he was staggering towards the car. Then, I had witnessed an incident with great astonishment. As soon as Beruni reached near the place, he gathered his last strength, dashed towards the car, and rummaged through some boxes. To my bewilderment, he took out a bottle of Stolichnaya, and started to gulp the vodka direct from its bottle. I raised my hands and uttered;

"Oh my God, the Most Gracious and the Most Merciful . . . . Please forgive my friend for his sin . . . . You have made this poor soul to suffer extreme cold . . . . and he could have perished . . . . May this vodka relieve some of his pain and suffering . . . .", I broke into laughter before I could finish the sentences.

It was his first and last hunting trip with me. After that he never asked to be taken on any hunting expedition. However, he did join me in picnics at the countryside for a few times after that. At one of the picnics, Beruni cut open a watermelon and scooped out the flesh and made a helmet out of the melon's shell as he walked around with it; much to the amusement of my children. We still kept the funny photo in our family album.

Ten years after I left Kazakhstan, I met Beruni again in Tripoli, Libya. He retired from the Foreign Ministry, and worked as a Consultant in a Korean Construction company that was developing a coastal resort near Tripoli. He took me to his country-house on the shore of the Mediterranean Sea, which was about 100 km away from Tripoli. We did a lot of reminiscing about happy old times. Then, he started talking about the uneasiness of the Libyan people towards Kaddafi and the ruling elites. At that time, it never occurred to me that such a powerful regime would succumb to the people's uprising.

I have a lot of other interesting stories about my hunting expeditions, with the company of other remarkable personalities such as Sultan Hayat Khan, the Ambassador of Pakistan, who scaled the Tien Shan mountain range on horseback with me, and Ruzi, the Afghan's Charge d' Affaires, who was always drunk in the trips. During one of the hunting trips, as soon as we left him alone, he was so intoxicated that he kept setting fire to the hunting ground. In another occasion, he fell from the boat into the freezing water, and blamed me furiously for that incident. After that, I stopped taking him along with me.

Chapter 27

Polysilicon Plant in Tashkumyr

I n the year 2000, the famous Malaysian Prime Minister
then, Tun Dr Mahathir Mohammed, visited the Kyrgyz
Republic, accompanied by huge entourage and business
delegation. I was summoned to the Kyrgyz capital, Bishkek
to assist the visiting delegation from my station in Almaty,
Kazakhstan. The Kyrgyz Republic was headed by soft-spoken
President Akaev (ousted in 2005 during "Tulip Revolution").

Tun Dr Mahathir was greatly admired by leaders of
the developing nations, including the newly independent
republics of Central Asia. He was hailed as one of the
most progressive state leaders with clear vision, who has
transformed Malaysia from an average agricultural state into
one of Asia's economic tigers. Tun Dr Mahathir was well
received by the Central Asian leaders, and the former loved
to be glorified.

And President Akaev was one of those smart persons
who capitalized this situation to the advantage of his
economically strapped republic. During one of the evening
chats between the two leaders at a secluded guest house at
the foot of Ala Archa mountain, which had lasted until wee
hour in the morning, President Akaev managed to secure

numerous financial and technical assistance from the Malaysian Prime Minister in just one night. What Akaev did was merely praising Tun Dr Mahathir and his brilliant policies throughout the evening that if a person ego was like filling up a balloon with air, Mahathir's head would have exploded due to excessive flattering.

Nevertheless, Mahathir's ego could not match the Uzbek President's, Islam Karimov. During a banquet held in honour of Tun Dr Mahathir's official visit to Uzbekistan, President Karimov literally cut short the Former's speech, as the Malaysian PM was about to tell how Uzbekistan could emulate Malaysia's formula in order to achieve strong economic growth. I remember, Mahathir was about the shift into fast gear in his speech or rather "preach", when suddenly President Karimov stood up and proposed that he would like to present some gifts to the Malaysian Prime Minister. One of the famous traditions was of course the presentation of an Uzbek traditional costume *cholpon*, a long robe made of velvet, embroidered with golden thread. President Karimov had personally put on the long robe on Tun Dr Mahathir, accompanied by the donning of traditional Uzbek scull cap. Although Tun Dr Mahathir's features did not differ that much from the Uzbeks, nevertheless, he looked rather awkward in the Uzbek robe. In short, without uttering, the Uzbek President had said;

". . . . Look, this is my country, Uzbekistan and I know how to run it without you telling me what to do . . . ."

Contrary to the Uzbek President, Akaev was such a humble person and had effectively used his charm to overwhelm Tun Dr Mahathir and in the end received numerous financial and technical assistance for his country. Following the visit, Malaysia had dispatched its experts to the Kyrgyz Republic to undertake various economic studies which would be funded under the Malaysian Technical Corporation Program (MTCP). The following morning, the visiting Prime Minister was sat on a helicopter and was taken to the mountainous area by his host in Ferghana Valley, to a secluded town in Jalalabad Oblast, called Tashkumyr.

GAO Kristall (literally translated as Government Auctioned Enterprise of Polysilicon) was an enormous industrial complex built by the USSR regime to produce polysilicon, basic raw material in the semiconductor industry. From polysilicon, monosilicon is produced, and then monosilicon is turned into wafers, which are used in various semiconductors. The Soviet Union intended to build this city to match the Silicon Valley in the United States. However, the disintegration of the USSR has derailed this ambitious plan, leaving the huge complex in the hand of Kyrgyz officials who didn't know what to do with it. Some of the parts such as ratification columns and other equipment which could be dismantled were quietly sold to China.

Currently, polysilicon is produced in three countries, namely the USA, Japan and Germany. The USSR used to have a small production facility in Poddolks, near Moscow but the plant was no longer safe and stopped its production decades ago. This particular site in Kyrgyz mountain was chosen because it met three most important criteria in the production of polysilicon; cheap electricity to run its massive complex, uninterrupted cold water supply to chill its production plant, and sufficient oxygen supply. Tashkumyr was located in the mountain pass separating the Uzbek and Kyrgyz sides of Ferghana Valley. A prominent river which originated from the nearby mountain range called Naryn runs through this area. There were at least three hydroelectric power stations built by the Russian scientists along the river, which produced the cheapest electricity in the world, as claimed by the Kyrgyzs. At the same time, the water temperature of Naryn is 0 Degree Celsius throughout the year, which makes it perfect to chill the production plant. As the site is located between two mountain ranges, the area became a natural wind pass, which provide sufficient oxygen supply for the plant.

After the main complex of the polysilicon plant was completed, the Soviet empire collapsed before it had time to be commissioned. The plant was inherited by the newly independent Kyrgyz Republic. Initially, the Kyrgyz would like to invite the Chinese Scientists to take over the plant. However, the Russians issued a stern warning to the Kyrgyz to keep away from the Chinese. A Japanese conglomerate, SUMITOMO Corporation quickly seized the opportunity to offer financial assistance to the Kyrgyz to initiate the production of polysilicon samples. I was told that the Kyrgyz officials involved in this project only used a small portion of SUMITOMO fund to produce the samples, while remaining balance were plundered and divided among the officials. However, they managed to produce some samples of solar grade which was handed to SUMITOMO.

Anyway, due to certain reasons, SUMITOMO did not pursue the collaboration with the Kyrgyz. When I established contact with SUMITOMO officials later on, I learnt that the Japanese decided not to pursue their intention due to immense bureaucracies and red tapes, as well as rampant corruption among the Kyrgyz Officials. The Japanese were astounded to see how its fund was plundered by the officials without justification. For more than two years, the polysilicon plant in Tashkumyr stood idle, as the population of the small town was rendered jobless. They were moved into this secluded place in the mountain specifically to work at this plant. For over two years, they didn't receive any salaries when the plant stopped its activities after SUMITOMO left. The Directors and other management staff, who were also deprived of their salaries, begun to dismantle some parts and sold them in the black market as scrap metal.

Suddenly came the savior, in the form of the Great Prime Minister of Malaysia. Tun Dr Mahathir was taken around the complex by President Akaev. Without much effort, Akaev managed to secure some funds from Dr Mahathir for the plant. The Economic Planning Unit (EPU) under Prime Minister's Department was immediately instructed to provide the fund while MIMOS Berhad, a government-back ICT company was designated to undertake the task as implementing agency to look into this project.

About two months after the visit, MIMOS "scientists" who neither had any formal education, nor experience in polysilicon production, were dispatched to the Kyrgyz Republic. Those boys immediately faced various obstacles and difficulties as soon as they step on Kyrgyz soil. They had countered problems in office, as well as while walking on the streets. They were constantly harassed by local policemen. Once, while travelling on the road in Jalalabad region, they were stopped and taken to the police station, where the Police Chief had emptied all cash in their wallets (a few hundred US dollars). They wrote a complaint to the President's Office, which led to the sacking of the Police Chief. However, the officer was reinstated, after he managed to raise some fund to bribe the Minister of Internal Affairs.

When MIMOS officials arrived in Tashkumyr, they discovered the horrible condition of the toilets at the plant, and quickly suggested some refurbishment job to be done. I was told that for over two months, the Malaysians were engaged in bitter quarrels over the exorbitant price quoted by the Kyrgyz partners for the toilet renovation. There were many other prominent issues, such as the missing parts of the plant production lines, as well as tussles over who was suppose to handle the procurement process. Nothing was achieved after six months of their presence, and MIMOS had almost given up their hope to work in the project.

At one of the coordination meetings organized by the EPU (Economic Planning Unit, PM's Department) at Putrajaya,[48] MIMOS's representatives at the meeting complained about various obstacles they faced in the Kyrgyz Republic. A friend of mine, who happened to attend the particular meeting suggested to MIMOS to hire a person who could speak the local language and understood the mentality, culture and tradition of Central Asian people to address the problems. MIMOS representative then asked where they could find such a person . . . .

A week after the EPU meeting, I took a short holiday to visit my parents in my hometown in Kedah. At that time I was serving in Almaty, Kazakhstan and just received a transfer order from the HQ to return home. My friend who attended the EPU coordination meeting had organized for me to meet the Managing Director of MySem Sdn Bhd, a subsidiary of MIMOS Berhad. He had to postpone his trip to his hometown in Kelantan to suit my itinerary. It was a *malam raya* (the night of 1st *Shawal* or *Eid ul Fitr*, when Muslims just completed their one month of fasting). We met at Petaling Jaya Hilton and had a lengthy talk. On that particular night, I was offered a contract "To Manage the

---

[48] *Putrajaya* is a planned city, located 25 km south of Kuala Lumpur, that serves as the federal administrative centre of Malaysia.

Project to Produce the Samples of Polysilicon at Tashkumyr Plant in Kyrgyz Republic".

I said I was not a scientist, but having served in the region for over 12 years, I have a small knowledge of the Central Asian people. In order to formalize my contract, MIMOS had sought permission from the government (Public Service Department) to employ me on a Secondment Contract (on loan). I departed for Kyrgyz Republic in March 2001.

The first thing that I did was to call for a meeting with the Top Management of GAO Kristall in Kyrgyz capital, Bishkek. During that first meeting, I told my Kyrgyz partners point blank in their language that my task was very simple. I was asked by the Malaysian government to assist them to produce polysilicon samples at Tashkumyr plant and if I failed to get cooperation from them, I shall close MIMOS office, say farewell and return home. In response, the plant's Director remarked that he was told that I had some experience working in the region and asked how long I had spent there. I replied;

". . . . very short period, it's only about 12 years . . .", said I.

"That's very long!", exclaimed the Director.

"Well . . . . I am afraid not long enough to fully understand the local people and I have a lot more to learn from them . . . .", I quipped.

After the brief introduction, I sought their stand if they were willing to work with me. When they gave their words, I moved straight into business.

". . . . First, let us start with the toilet renovation . . . .", I said as my eyes were busily searching for the figures in the quotation which was handed to me by the plant's Director. He told me that it was the agreed sum accepted by my Predecessor for the job, USD 1,500.

In response, I suggested that a Notice to be placed at a local Bazaar in Tashkumyr town inviting prospective local contractors to undertake the job for US $ 250, with a caption that cash payment in US currency shall be made upon completion of the job. The Kyrgyz were visibly stunned by my suggestion. However, they agreed to implement it. (Later, I learnt that a day after the notice was out, scores of local foremen scrambled at the office, bidding for the job).

Before leaving for the Kyrgyz Republic, I had requested for a detailed briefing by my Predecessor. I was fully prepared when I met the Kyrgyz. I was enjoying every bit of the moment, as I continued sizing up my partners by revealing one after another about their hidden agenda behind every move they made that have frustrated my Predecessor. At the end of the meeting, I appealed to them to look at the long term objectives, instead of short-term gains. The Kyrgyz were visibly dumb founded after their first meeting with me.

We rented a small office on the premise belonging to the State Geological Department. It was a quiet place, located in a small garden behind the main building hidden from the public view. It served as the MIMOS Representative Office in Bishkek. After I found a modest house at the edge of the city, I moved out from the Hotel and quickly settled down. It was the time to visit the plant about 500 km away from the Capital.

Tashkumyr is situated about 500 km from Bishkek. It could have been a shorter distance if we did not have to circle Toktogul Lake (a ferry service would have been a good solution). However, due to the poor road conditions, as well as the rugged topography of the territory, it took us more than 12 hours to travel by car from the Kyrgyz capital under normal circumstances. One hour after we passed a small town, Kara-Balta, we begin to ascend Kyrgyz Range where we would meet a 2 km long tunnel, dug into the mountain which was very dangerous for travellers, especially during winter. The road surface on the other side of the tunnel was always frozen during winter, and was extremely dangerous.

During that time, busses were prohibited from using that road, after a horrible accident that killed all passengers in a bus which plunged into the rocky ravine and swept away by freezing water. Two years before, a much worse accident occurred, when hundreds of travellers suffocated and perished, after massive traffic jam happened in the tunnel. They were trapped for hours in the tunnel when the exit road was blocked by an overturned truck. All of the victims died of poisonous gas emitted from their own vehicles (exhaust pipes).

Twice, I had to travel on this road during winter and on both occasions, I met with road accidents. During the first year, my Russian-made 4WD spinned around two circles on the slippery road before it hit the mountain slope. We were lucky because our vehicle did not plunge into the ravine 100 meters below, where the passengers of the fateful bus met their tragedy.

During the second year, we were travelling under heavy snowfall. I was feeling so tired and sleepy, having driven for over 12 hours under such dreadful condition. Therefore, I handed the steering wheel to my local assistant, Aibek, a young man in his late 20's. Before I could fully adjust my seat into a comfortable position, our car suddenly "flew" off the road, and landed on a heap of rocks. Apparently, Aibek could not see the sharp band as he drove the vehicle off the road. Indeed, it was very difficult to determine whether you were on the right track or headed for the roadside drain, as the surrounding area looked like a white borderless field.

The heavy snowfall from morning which lasted till late evening had covered the road surface and surrounding areas. There was no street light what so ever on the deserted road. Nevertheless, we made it safely to Tashkumyr, after 18 hours despite the accident and rough journey.

There was a small settlement before we ascended to the higher ground leading to Tashkumyr. On the right side was Naryn River, running noisily at some places. Its surface was glistering when our headlights hit the water. There were a few dimly-lit cafes erected along the road, facing the Naryn. We stopped at one of the small cafes and ordered grilled mountain trout, freshly caught from the nearby river. It was truly amazing. Apparently, the place was famous for this specialty, and most travellers passing this place would not miss the opportunity to savour the grilled fish or quail birds cooked with local herbs.

Having narrowly escaped horrific accident twice, I decided not to travel to Tashkumyr during winter, but instead to visit the place frequently during the summer. It was more relaxing and fun to travel during summer as we could see beautiful and unique landscapes, especially along the Naryn. However, there was a small problem travelling during summer, as we would be stopped numerous times by the traffic police along the journey. These policemen would find every excuse to solicit payment from you. They would simply accused you of speeding, or asking stupid questions such as why our plate number was yellow in colour instead of black and white like others (yellow plate number was accorded to business expatriates' vehicles). The Policemen would open the booth and asked if we have the permit to carry the items in our trunk, even if they didn't know anything about the stuff. If they could not find any fault, then they would ask if we have any souvenirs for them.

Since petrol kiosk was very scarce on this road (if any, they only offered low octane petrol), we always take along spare gasoline in canisters. Most of the Policemen who happened to open the booth would have strong temptation to take away one of the containers, much to the chagrin of my local assistant

"Why didn't you protest Sir?" asked Aibek when one of the Policemen at the roadblock took away a canister of our petrol.

I told Aibek it was alright, as he took something that I have in excess. I said probably he needed it badly and in the process, the man did not insult my pride. I assured Aibek that the Policemen would remember us and indeed, on the way back we met a roadblock manned by the same Policeman. He waved us away the moment he recognized our car. However, I stopped and handed him a packet of peaches I bought from the mountain as a good gesture. From that moment, he never gave us any trouble.

During one of my trips to Tashkumyr, I hid a hunting riffle in the booth. I brought the rifle with me from my previous station, Kazakhstan where I had a license for it. But that license was issued by the Kazakhstan government. I know that I would end up in a slight trouble, if the local Policemen happened to find out about the rifle and started to ask for the license. My fear turned into reality.

There were two junctions after we passed Kara-Kol town, one leading to Talas Oblast and the other to Tashkumyr. There was a permanent roadblock set up at this strategic junction. If you happened to pass the junction when the Policemen were busy inspecting fully loaded trucks, you may escape the roadblock, unnoticed. However, when we arrived at the checkpoint that day, the road was almost deserted, probably due to excessive heat of hot summer day. The

Policemen under the scorching sun pointed his striped black and white baton to our car and signalled us to stop.

I begun to recite some prayers taught by my father when you were under such circumstances. First, the Policeman examined my driving license. When everything was in order, he asked for the registration card of my vehicle, which also happened to be in order. Then the Policeman ordered me to open the booth. He started to ransack through our luggage as if looking for something. Just as the Policeman was about to flip up the compartment of the spare tire where I hid the riffle, I drew his attention to the petrol canister and asked him where the next petrol kiosk is. He told me in Tashkumyr town, about 120 km away. I pretended to ask Aibek if our reserve of 3 canisters would be sufficient for us. Having understood my real intention, Aibek replied that a canister would be more than what we need to reach Tashkumyr. He straightaway suggested that I presented a canister to the Policeman since we have additional spare. The stern-looking Policeman gave a sweetest smile of the day, and totally forgot about his intention to check the spare-tire compartment. I inhaled a deep breath, and winked at Aibek with a relief smile too.

Every time I passed the winding road close to Tashkumyr, as an ardent hunter, I always noticed about the presence of flocks of wild *kiklik* (a larger species of quail birds) inhibiting mountainous area or high hills. That was the reason why I brought the riffle with me to Tashkumyr. Indeed, on that particular trip, we had a special dish of stewed *kikliks*, cooked with young potatoes for our dinner. When reaching the particular pass where the flocks of *kikliks* used to cross, I took out and loaded the riffles with cartridges. From inside the car, I fired at the birds, as they flew across the road, while Aibek scrambled out to fetch the fallen games.

As we negotiated the winding roads, on the bank of Naryn, we experienced a mixed feeling between the joy of witnessing one of the most spectacular panoramas, and the fear of falling into strong current of Naryn deep down below. Therefore, we always kept our vehicle close to the left side. It was better to hit the jaggered rocks than falling into ice-cold river. Sometimes, the wind was so strong that we had to stop our car and wait until the gust of wind subsides, before we could continue on our journey. There were cases where small cars were swept by the strong winds into the river.

Tashkumyr Polysilicon Complex could be seen from afar, as we approached the town. It was a gigantic construction with tall ratification columns built close to the Naryn River. During my first arrival to Tashkumyr, I had driven pass by the complex, but did not stop as it was already late. It was about 8.00 pm, however, the day was still bright as it was summer time. After a brief glance at the factory, we headed for the rest house. I was met by two Malaysian staff from MIMOS, who were stationed there a couple of months earlier. We got to know each other and settled for a simple dinner. The rented house was fine based on local standard. It was small but cozy with rose garden and vegetable plots in the courtyard. The only thing I didn't like was the location of the toilet. Similar to other traditional Central Asian homes, the toilet of this house was built outside the home. In winter, you have to endure chilly weather should you want to ease yourself in the middle of the night.

The following morning, after a hefty breakfast of freshly baked "non" (flat bread) and leftover oily lamb kabob from last night's dinner, home-made yogurt and dried fruits, we headed for the plant. I was met by the Director and the entire staff of Tashkumyr plant. They gathered at the entrance since morning, I was told, to welcome new "boss" from Malaysia who could speak local languages, as the words spread around. They formed a long line as soon as our car entered the factory compound. I witnessed happy faces and felt their elevated spirit. Soon I realized that they had great expectation from me.

I was introduced to the key personnel of the plant. Some names that I could remember were of course Jarasul, the Director, Samerkin, the Deputy, Panarbek, the Chief Engineer, and Zamir, Procurement Manager of Uzbek descendant. After shaking hands with everybody (on that day I felt like a celebrated politician), I was taken around to inspect the entire plant. First of all I had requested to see the newly renovated toilet, much to the amusement of those presence. I wanted to see the toilet which had caused so much problem and almost derailed the entire project. Apparently, it was an ordinary toilet in the former Soviet Union. A simple job to repaint and replace broken bowl, as well as some floor scrubbing job would have rendered it useable and I concluded that $ 250 was just a fair fee for the job.

There were various sections of the plant; each large was enough to be an independent unit. There was a special plant to generate oxygen, a separate plant to produce special crystal bowls which could stand extraordinary high temperature, in which polysilicon is "grown". Special silica sand, imported all the way from Norway was heated at high temperature until it turned into liquid and baked or "grown" in those crystal bowls for weeks, until it became a cylinder shape polysilicon. There was also a hydrogen plant. I was told that it has an extremely cold nitrogen gas chamber, which could churn human body into crystal dust if a person happened to fall into the chamber. The recounting really scared me off.

Since I did not have any background in physic like the engineers from MIMOS, I had to take additional effort to read some materials available only in Russian language about polysilicon production. In this respect, I had the advantage over those engineers who didn't know the language. Furthermore, I also could freely engage in conversations with the local experts about the industry. Soon, I was asked to lead the briefing when we returned home to MIMOS Headquarters to present the progress report on the project, even on technical matters. As a matter of fact, with the help from Klichbae[49], a year later I had enrolled for a post-graduate study (Masters degree) at one of Moscow technical universities majoring in "polysilicon production process". I decided to do that because a leading scientist at the Russian Academy of Sciences had promised to allocate 3 places for PhD degrees, with the introduction of his newly invented technology at GAO Kristall plant. Inspired to bid for one of the doctorate seats, I must have a strong basis in that respective field. Sadly, I never completed the study.

One of the things that captured my attention was The Master Plan for the Development of Tashkumyr Town, prepared by the Soviet government, which was displayed at the Director's Conference Hall. Based on the original plan, Tashkumyr would have 250,000 populations, many among them were skilled and semi-skilled workers. Among the infrastructure planned for the town were the construction

---

[49] The writer's local technical advisor who was educated in Moscow and once served as Science Advisor to President Akaev.

of 4 schools, scores of kindergartens, 2 universities, 2 stadiums and other sports and recreational facilities, public hospitals and shopping malls. It was supposed to be a modern town to suit its function as the Soviet "silicon valley". However, before the grand plan could be executed, the Empire collapsed, leaving the ailing newly independent republic helplessly struggled to continue with the project.

Coming back to the missing items from the plant, my greatest challenge was to find replacement for the stolen items and spare parts. When I received the quotations for those missing items from our partners in remarkably record breaking time, I began to suspect something amiss. It would take a couple of weeks to prepare the long list of the required parts and to get the quotations from the suppliers. I would say they would have been a bunch of highly efficient managers if they could deliver the quotations within one and the half months. However, in less than two weeks, the quotations were already on my table. Having examined the list of suppliers, I noticed that most of those suppliers had their registered offices either in Tashkumyr or the nearest town, Jalalabad. One could not help but to admire the fact that these small towns were thrive with suppliers of spare parts for such precisely designed plant and equipment.

However, instead of questioning the integrity of my local partners on their dubious quotations, which would lead to their further resentment, I accepted the quotations, and commended them for the extraordinary speedy job. However, I quietly dispatched my trusted assistants, Aibek and Klichbae to run a check up on the background of those so-called suppliers. It took them only two days to confirm my suspicion that most of the suppliers were "dummy" companies set up for this purpose, and some were genuine companies which belonged to friends or relatives of the members of the plant's top management. None of those suppliers have any experience in supplying spare parts for a polysilicon plant. A few were involved in the supply of melons, fruits and vegetables from Jalalabad region to Bazaars in Bishkek.

Having informed my partners that I would study the quotations, I returned to Bishkek and on the following day, took a flight to Moscow, accompanied by Klichbae, whom I recruited as my Technical Advisor. Klichbae was a scientist who graduated from one of the most prestigious universities in Russia. He was an expert in laser technology and attached to the Chernobyl nuclear plant during the catastrophe. As a result of that disaster, Klichbae also suffered some physical effects and received an "invalid" card which carried small privileges such as access to special medical treatment and a small pension.

After his extensive medical treatment in Moscow, following the Chernobyl disaster, Klichbae return to Bishkek as a hero and appointed as President's Advisor on Science & Technology. He was given a large office in the same building where President Akaev was. Sadly, it was a high position with no specific job. Anyway, what would you do with a laser technology expert in a republic saddled with acute economic trouble? Therefore, when he learnt about our arrival, Klichbae volunteered himself to assist us in our job without asking how much his remuneration would be.

I was lucky to have Klichbae around, as he still could remember some factories and production enterprises around Moscow where we could source for the parts for the Tashkumyr plant. He still had some valuable contacts in strategic offices where we could ask for assistance. Sometimes, his friends sent their cars with driver to take us from one corner of the city to another. Otherwise, we would travel by underground METRO or a taxi. In a week, we managed to secure the quotations of the required parts direct from the manufacturers.

On the night before we departed for Bishkek, I treated Klichbae at one of famous Uzbek restaurants in Moscow and managed to pull a trick at the old man. After the marvellous dinner, we took a stroll at Arbat Street, and took a great pleasure to examine various work of arts by local artists and craftsmen. As we arrived at the end of the street, I notice a signboard "Las Vegas Striptease Club", written in English at one of the nightclubs. I knew Klichbae would not take the trouble to read what was written in English. As he was admiring a beautiful set of brightly painted *matrushka*[50] from one of the street peddlers, I quietly slipped into the nightclub and bought a ticket. Then I went to find my friend, and led him by the hand into the nightclub. As he was trying to figure out where he was, I told him that we were sitting in one of the best comedy theatres, and advised him to enjoy the show while I would be meeting a friend in a nearby street. I hurriedly left the puzzled man.

When I was done browsing in a large bookstore on the Gorky Street about an hour later, I returned to the nightclub where I had left my friend. He was already standing on the staircase at the entrance waiting for me. The man grasped his head with both hands as soon as he saw me.

"Comedy you said . . . .", he lamented as we broke into laughter.

Klichbae left Moscow before Russia embarked on market economy and embraced free enterprise. Soon, after the changes took place, the city of Moscow was transformed

---

[50] Brightly painted wooden dolls which reveals a separate unit of another smaller figures inside each of it.

into one of the lively cities of the world, with the emergence of newly rich elites displaying their extravagant lifestyle. Casinos and exclusive clubs were established at every street corner. It was a cultural shock for people like Klichbae. I just wanted to expose him about the new world, an environment that is totally different from the one he used to live under the socialism. It was so that later, we could indulge into discussions about the pros and cons of the two systems. It was the first striptease show that he ever saw. Anyway, he said he didn't fancy it very much. "Perhaps it's the side effect from Chernobyl", I further amused the old man. Before returning to our hotel, I took him to have a look inside one of the casinos on the Arbat Street. He was visibly confused to see how some people could gamble and part away with large amount of money without any sign of profound regret. I told him that they were addicted to gambling, similar to people who got addicted to drugs. They have lost all their senses. Anyway, there were people who became sore losers and sometimes lost their tempers as well, when they lost in the black jack, roulettes or poker games, I told Klichbae.

Klichbae was such a naive and straightforward person. He narrated to me that as a kid, he lived in an isolated home on the mountain in Jalalabad region. His father worked as a ranger in the Forestry Department. There were abundant of walnuts trees around the house. As their house was very far from town or provision shops, her mother had made full use of the walnuts in her cooking. Walnuts bread, walnuts onion soup, walnuts salad, salted walnuts, walnuts soaked in honey. Since everything had walnuts that he thought walnuts was the country's staple food, and the world would probably fall apart without walnuts. Klichbae only discovered about other gastronomic dishes without walnuts, when his father sent him to a boarding school in Jalalabad.

When we returned to Bishkek, I called for a meeting with the plant's top management to decide on the procurement of the spare parts. I observed that the Director and his right-hand men were so excited that morning. On the tables, in front of everyone, there were quotations presented by the plant's Director. As soon as everyone was ready, I passed around another set of quotations we brought back from Moscow and allowed a couple of minutes of silence, while I studied the body language of my Kyrgyz partners. Honestly, they were in the state of horror and shock. Firstly, they never expected that there would be another quotations. Secondly, my quotation was between 35-50 percent cheaper than the lowest quotation that they had presented to me.

When I thought that my Kyrgyz partners had regained their composure, I said that I would allow the Director to make the decision to choose the suppliers. If he decided to pick up the lowest offer, than we could straight away confirm our order with the Moscow suppliers. However, if the Director felt that the contract should be given to the second or third lowest quotations, then he must forward his justification to MIMOS in Kuala Lumpur. After a brief silence, the Director, in sombre voice agreed that we source the parts directly from Moscow. Without showing any sign of joy, I silently celebrated my victory, adjourned the meeting, and invited them for lunch at nearby café. Although the Turkish cuisines served at the café were sumptuous, they did not seem to enjoy the food very much and became less talkative that day. I assigned Zamir to undertake the procurement process.

I thought I have outsmarted the Kyrgyz, only to find out that they were a bunch of shrewd people. After three weeks, Zamir reported to me that they have received all the parts.

Once again, I was astonished at the speed of their work. I was told by Moscow suppliers that some of the items must be fabricated to meet our specifications, meaning that it would take a month or two for us to receive the order. I dispatched Aibek to investigate. In the evening, I received the feedback which astounded me greatly . . . . Apparently, Zamir had contacted all Moscow suppliers and informed that they have been selected to supply the parts. However, they didn't have to deliver the parts as all the required parts were already delivered to the plant. Moscow suppliers were only required to submit dummy invoices and bill of ladings, in exchange with certificate of acknowledgement receipt from the plant signed by no other than Zamir himself. The Moscow suppliers would be rewarded with 5 percent of the contract value for their cooperation. At that time, most of traders in Russia and CIS preferred to accept cash payment, preferably in foreign currency, instead of payment through banks. In our case, I just handed cash payment to Zamir, every time he submitted the invoice and the slip of acknowledge receipt as a proof that the ordered parts have been delivered.

That was how I came to know what happened after SUMITOMO had left. Apparently, some parts of the plant were stripped off from their positions and kept at one of the scoundrels' store (many suspected at Mr Samerkin's garage). Nevertheless, I decided not to do anything about it, as long as all the parts were there to enable us to start the production. Opening up the case would lead to a scandal or probably derailment of the project.

While the works to re-install the parts were undertaken, I placed orders for silica sand from Norway, and the shipment of trikhlorsilan (chlorine), a hazardous material from Tatarstan. The task to bring the material proven to be very challenging. First, we had to order a special container for hazardous material. Then we had to seek approval from railway authorities of neighbouring Kazakhstan and Uzbekistan to allow an express train to pass through their territories. The train should not stop at any station during the three day journey, as the temperature of the hazardous gas might rise up and cause catastrophic explosion. Thirdly, we had to arrange for the services of heavily armed Russian commandoes to escort the cargo from Moscow to Tashkumyr.

Finally, our hard works paid off, as on the designated day, the polysilicon plant started its production process without any untoward incident. The Director suggested that a black sheep needed to be sacrificed in the historic morning. Luckily we didn't have to sacrifice any scapegoat involved in the stolen parts.

I truly cherished the experience in this entirely new arena. During the course of managing this project, I had the opportunities to attend various meetings and seminars on this subject, as well as having the privilege to know some people in this exclusive circle of polysilicon business. I noticed that there were many parties who were interested in our activities and ever ready to meet us. However, the best opportunity of all was the chance to meet Professor Prokhorov, a world renowned figure in polysilicon industry.

Professor M. Prokhorov was one of the most outstanding personalities at the Russian Academy of Sciences. Born in Australia in 1916, his family migrated to USSR in 1923. He graduated from Leningrad State University, and continued his study in Moscow until he completed his PhD in "Coherent Radiation of Electrons in the Synchorotron Accelerator". Prof Prokhorov, who was an expert in laser technology, then expanded his research in polysilicon production. In 1964, he was awarded the Nobel Prize in physics for his contribution to science. I wouldn't stand a small chance to come near to this man if not for Klichbae, who happened to be one of his favourite students. As soon as I knew about this relationship, I asked Klichbae to arrange our visit to the top Russian scientist at his office at the Academy of Sciences in Moscow. Prior to the visit, I had studied the document entitled "The Production of Polysilicon in Closed Cycle". It was the hot stuff written by the professor. It was a revolutionary technology to produce polysilicon.

Polysilicon production was highly hazardous and harmful to the environment. Therefore, only three countries in the world were producing this material. Prokhorov's new technology would address the main concern of the environmentalists, as under this method, chlorine would not be discharged and instead recycled. Presently, chlorine was discharged as waste material to the atmosphere and caused environmental degradation. This new technology would greatly improve the situation. We understood that secret agents of certain foreign governments were eager to have an access to this technology.

I was a little nervous due to excitement, when I walked into Prokhorov's Office. We were met by three scientists who were close friend of Klichbae. They were serving the Professor as Personal Assistants on special projects. Minutes later a tall, lean figure of an old man entered the room as we rose from our chairs to greet him. A charismatic Professor Prokhorov was over 85 years when I met him. He recognized Klicbae and asked about the present affairs of his former student. Klichbae then introduced me, so and so from Malaysia as the witty professor quickly retorted;

". . . . Well, apparently there is such a country . . . ."

Soon I found myself at ease and begun to probe him with some questions about "The Closed Cycled Method". At the same time, I was really worried if the great scientist would engage into deep technical conversations as I was merely a pretender. I didn't like physics, and barely passed the subject during the high school examination. Suddenly the Professor popped up a question;

".... Which silicon plant did you say you had worked before going to Kyrgyzia?"

"I didn't say anything .... as a matter of fact I could hardly repair a bicycle, let alone working at a polysilicon plant, except as a janitor. I am just interested in that shiny, glittery thing...", I responded

Prokhorov just smiled at me and paused for a few seconds. Then he asked what I really wanted to know, as he observed me with his sharp penetrating eyes.

"Well .... I want to know if we could fix your newly invented Closed Cycle Technology at Tashkumyr plant.....".

"Do you want me to pass my technology to the Kyrgyz? Hell no! I'm sorry Klichbae ... but I really don't trust the Kyrgyz ....", said he without mincing his words. Then he continued;

"Unless...."

"Unless we took over GAO Kristall?", I quipped.

"Precisely .... and that's my condition", added the Professor.

I turned to look at Klichbae, who nodded his head. Then, I drew the attention of Prokhorov's three assistants, and declared in a loud clear voice;

"Listen guys .... you are my witnesses that our professor has agreed to give his new technology to the Malaysian company".

Professor Prokhorov was already 85 years old at that time. If he happened to die, I need an assurance from his assistants that they would honour the promise made by their chief. (Indeed, the following year the great professor passed away peacefully in his sleep on January 6, 2002 at the age of 86).

I enquired about the estimated cost to install the new production plant with this technology, which the Professor responded around US 100 million. I left the Russian Academy of Sciences a happy man.

Words soon spread among the players of polysilicon industry about my meeting with Professor Prokhorov. One of the most enthusiastic parties was E, a Norwegian company, a leading trader of polysilicon and monosilicon. The company's Representative in Moscow has been very active to cultivate business relations with us. He would offer to fetch me from the airport when I visited the city. As anticipated, one fine day, he raised the subject of my meeting with Prokhorov. I hinted to him that there was a strong possibility to see this new technology fixed at Tashkumyr plant. The guy told me that E was very interested to collaborate with MIMOS on this new technology. The E representative asked me about the estimated cost to construct the new technology, and I responded that US 200 million would be sufficient. Didn't you see that I also could be a shrewd businessman? He remarked that it was a very reasonable sum because recently a Japanese firm quoted US 250 million to build a production plant for a German company, bearing in mind that Prokhorov's technology was revolutionary.

The following week I returned to Kuala Lumpur for a short holiday. I received a call from one of E top officials from Oslo who sought an appointment with me. I told him that I had a rather tight schedule and suggested that we could meet in Moscow in 10 days time as I would be going there. However, he was very persistent to see me as soon as possible in Kuala Lumpur. Finally, I agreed to meet him at a Transit Hotel at KLIA as requested by him.

The Norwegian showed up at the KLIA Pan Pacific Hotel right on the appointed hour and went straight into business. He told me that E was ready to become MIMOS partner at GAO Kristall and willing to invest US 200 million to secure Prokhorov's new technology. The proposed equity was 50-50 and subject to further discussion, should MIMOS felt that the company must hold the majority shares. The only condition set by E was that MIMOS must take over the plant from the Kyrgyz government, the request which I personally felt was not impossible to accomplish. The E guy then handed a letter of intent from his company to me and took leave. I asked where he was going after this. He gave a very short reply "Back to Oslo". It touched me deeply about the seriousness of these people. They sent someone all the way from Oslo to Kuala Lumpur just to deliver a Letter of Intent.

Meanwhile, our work to grow polysilicon using the technology was moving on the right track. It was a little bit behind the schedule, but it could have been derailed altogether if not properly controlled. Everyone in the plant was excited when a small "seed" begun to emerge in the crystal bowl. The section of the plant where polysilicon was grown ran continuously non-stop for weeks. After several weeks of anxiety, we finally managed to grow six batons of polysilicon cylinders weighing about 6kg each. They were sent for testing at SUMITOMO's laboratory to determine its quality. While waiting for the test result, I took a short vacation with my family as I have been away for nearly a year working on this project.

The laboratory test from SUMITOMO shown that the polysilicon produced by GAO Kristall plant were of "solar grade". The highest grade of polysilicon is "electronic grade". I concluded my report for submission to MIMOS, as soon as we received the result of the laboratory test.

Sadly, when the report on GAO Kristall polycilicon samples was completed, MIMOS was at the state of chaos following the financial scandal, when it lost a lot of money invested in an asset management company called "METROWANGSA" (*Tabung Haji* or Muslim Pilgrimage Fund, another GLC also lost hundreds of million through similar investment scheme). Ironically, MIMOS was entrusted to lead R & D works on new technologies. However, other than becoming the pioneer in the transfer of screw-driver technology (assembling computers and laptops manufactured by Taiwan and sold it to the government offices (at very exorbitant price!), the organisation had used its allocations in dubious investment company.

At the same time, my boss, Managing Director of MySem was made a scapegoat on the failure of MIMOS "wafer" project. Hundreds of million were spent to produce sample of "wafers'" which would be acceptable by the prospective buyers, using obsolete technology provided by a Japanese company. It was like selling a Pentium II laptop to a computer-illiterate person, while the market has been flooded with Pentium IV product. After spending some time to learn about computer, only then the poor guy realised that he has been deceived. It would be too late to do anything, except to do what MIMOS has done, which was to pump more money to upgrade or catch up with fast moving technology.

When MIMOS CEO visited USA in 2002, he was taken by the host to a factory producing "wafers" of similar grade to what MIMOS was trying to achieve at home. In simple note, the American businessman made the offer to MIMOS to take over the whole factory "lock stock and barrel" for US 100 million.

"Save yourself from trouble trying to produce the sample. This factory is running at its maximum capacity".

What a big blow! MIMOS had at that time spent so much money just to produce the samples. I was told that one of Tun Mahathir's son was the supplier of the technology at MIMOS wafer project. Anyway, in normal mind, who would believe that MIMOS would be able to undertake such project when it has only two engineers working on the project? There were 6 team of engineers working at the US plant which was offered for sale to MIMOS and each team comprised of 6 engineers. Well, Malaysia Boleh.[51]

As customary to Malaysian tradition, a scapegoat must be found. This time the Managing Director of MySem who hired me was blamed for the failure. He was asked to resign. When he refused to do so, he was given an empty room with only a chair and table, without any task. After a couple of months, he grew tired of reading newspapers in his room and quit MIMOS. Meanwhile, The Financial Controller was sacked in relation with METROWANGSA scandal, despite the report made by Price Waterhouse stated that the decision to invest in METROWANGSA was made by the Board of Directors. The Financial Controller only carried out the decision made by the Board. I guess, after 10 years, the guy would become an instant millionaire when his case is heard in court.

I brought back the report on polysilicon project under the above circumstances. The former Managing Director of MySem could not do anything, as he was sitting in the

---

[51] A slogan campaign that carries the meaning "Malaysia Can!"

cold storage (it was really depressing to see a man who was stripped of his dignity, sitting alone in an isolated room of a warehouse). I approached his successor who was seconded from Hicom Berhad[52]. He said he was not interested in my project. When I pleaded to him he told me that his main task was to clean up MIMOS's financial mess. Secondly, he was not an engineer and knew nothing about the polysilicon. Thirdly, he said he was not in favour of investing abroad based on bad experience faced by PROTON which failed in all the countries it ventured in. I argued that polysilicon was not automobile industry. He responded that the earlier ground that he was not familiar with the subject. He suggested that I personally meet the CEO. I tried to seek an appointment but failed to see him until my last day at MIMOS.

When the Economic Planning Unit (EPU) of the Prime Minister's Department enquired if MIMOS would like to withdraw US 5 million allocations for the second phase of the project, the Latter replied that it did not intend to pursue further with the project, citing two reasons. Firstly, MIMOS did not have experts to manage the project and secondly, GAO Kristall could only produce "solar grade" polysilicon.

The first reason was indeed true although many solutions could be made if MIMOS really wanted to continue with the project. However, the second reason was truly misleading. As a matter of fact, more than 80 % of market demand was for "solar grade" polysilicon, while "electronic grade" only made up of less than 20% usage.

---

[52] HICOM is a Government-Linked Companies (GLC) and had been instrumental in leading the nation's drive towards industrialisation and among its major achievements was the development of the National Car Project.

Furthermore, MIMOS never mentioned in its short response to EPU that SUMITOMO was willing to buy 100% of GAO Kristall "solar grade" polysilicon. The Norwegian company E also expressed the same interest to become MIMOS sole distributor.

I didn't have any opportunity to tell that E has agreed to invest US 200 million in the project to fix new Prokhorov's Close Cycle Technology at Tashkumyr plant. I also could not tell that the Kyrgyz government has agreed to hand over the entire plant to MIMOS, with the conditions that we settle the plant's liabilities in back wages, outstanding debts to creditors and outstanding utility bills, all amounted to US $3 (Three) million, and to provide employment for residents of Tashkumyr. The Kyrgyz Deputy Prime Minister called me to his office and made the offer when they heard the possibility that MIMOS would pull out of the project. The Kyrgyz fully understood that the fate of the entire population of Tashkumyr depended on that plant.

I had planned to use part of the EPU's allocation of US 5 million to pay for the plant's liabilities and took over GAO Kristall, before inviting E to become new business partner, should MIMOS agreed to go ahead. Based on original plan, the EPU would allocate additional US 5 million for the commercialization of the project. The assets of the whole GAO Kristall complex was estimated at above US 150 million.

In 2007, I met Tun Dr Mahathir at the Perdana Foundation. At first, he thought I was a reporter (those were Pak Lah'[53]s bashing days and any reporter who sought

---

[53] Tun Abdullah bin Haji Ahmad Badawi or informally known as Pak Lah served as Prime Minister of Malaysia from 2003 to 2009.

appointments with him were welcomed). When I mentioned about his official visit to Kyrgyz Republic, the former PM recollected everything. I narrated the above story. The old statesman was visibly upset and said that he was not briefed on the whole scenario. In response I said,

". . . . Since when the government officers told you everything. They only told what you wanted to hear . . . ."

I dared to utter those comments because he was no longer the Prime Minister, and I was no longer working with the government.

In 2003, I was seconded by the Tourist Development Board to head its Moscow Office. One day, some Russian businessmen came to the office and sought my help to take them to Tashkumyr. They planned to take over the polysilicon plant. I applied for leave and flew to Kyrgyz with those Russians. After a brief inspection of the plant and holding consultations with some old friends there, I told the Russians to forget about the plant. The stolen parts could be recovered. However, the biggest problem was the fact that the Kyrgyz had compartmentalized the different sections of the plant, and privatized them to different people. It would be great headache to do business with those people. The Russians heeded my advice and never returned to Tashkumyr. GAO Kristall complex must be a haunted house now, or perhaps Tashkumyr has become a ghost town.

I shall always cherish those fond memories, great hospitality of the Kyrgyz people, especially Panarbek, the Chief Engineer who strived hard sincerely to ensure the success of the project. At the same time, I recalled amusing incidents during those two years. There was a man from the Kyrgyz Secret Service who was stationed in Tashkumyr. Every summer holiday, he would wait for days, sitting on a stool from morning till evening at the corner of our office in Bishkek, waiting for our Director to turn up. At this time, our Director would be very elusive too. When the secret service guy needed money to send his family for vacation at the Issykul Lake Resort, as the customary of the Kyrgyz people during summer, he would solicit money from our Director. I was told that the Secret Service guy from Tashkumyr had always blackmailed the Plant's Director. The Latter must have done some serious offence that he was subjected to such extortion all the time. He was harassed constantly when he visited Tashkumyr. He was ambushed at Bishkek Office every summer.

Ironically, GAO Kristall Director was accorded the rank of One Star General for his strategic position, and yet he was subdued by a lower ranking secret service man. The funny part was the scene the determination of the secret service man to nail our Director. On one occasion, we noticed that he sat for a whole week on a stool, waiting for our Director to turn up at office. Someone has alerted him about the presence of the secret service guy, so he did not turn up at office the whole week. Finally, the secret service guy approached me as I was leaving the office, and asked about the whereabout of the Director. I told him that I haven't heard from him for a week, and someone told me that the Director was having a vacation with his family in Issykul Resort. The Secret Service man was so exited and enquired further if I knew any particular resort. I said I did not have any knowledge of that. Later I learnt that the man indeed went to Issykul, and was frantically looking for the Director all over the place. As a matter of fact the Director was sitting quietly at his home, as that summer, he was totally broke and could not even dispatch his family for vacation, let alone pay the extortion money to the Tashkumyr guy.

Another thrilling moment was when I and Dr Uda, a visiting engineer from MIMOS were stopped by drunken policemen at one of the major streets in Bishkek. Prior to that, we passed-by a street peddler who sold a few items, among them was a 12 inch home-made knife. It was very sharp and was a bargain. Thinking that it would make a good butcher knife, I bought it, wrapped in old newspaper, and hid under my shirt. As we were walking pass a roadside café, two men rushed out or rather staggered out and shouted to us to stop. The smell of alcohol soon penetrated our nostrils. They claimed that they were policemen and demanded to see our documents. I demanded to see their authority card. Visibly annoyed, they nevertheless produced the police identity cards. One of them begun to examine Dr Uda's passport and the other started to body frisk my visiting friend who begun to tremble in fear, as the Policeman who examined his passport started to question the legality of his visa and threatened to take us to the Police Station for thorough examination. He suggested that we could have hidden some cocaine in our rectum.

I would have a field day of joy with those Policemen if not for the hidden knife tucked under my shirt. The Policemen then asked for Dr Uda's wallet and I told him not to surrender it if he didn't want to lose his cash. The annoyed Policemen turned to me and before he could frisk my body I yelled at him to leave us alone. I told him that we were invited by the government and if he continued to harass us I would shove his ass and report the matter direct to the Prime Minister. They were startled and never expected that I could scold them eloquently in Russian, complete with appropriate curses. Before the drunken Kyrgyz could regain their composure, I added;

"Now if you guys need money to continue with your booze, just ask nicely. We are nice people . . . . why do you have to harass and embarrass us in front of these crowds . . . . KAZEOL!"

"KAZEOL" in Russian is "GOAT". I guess different country used different animal to describe the stupidity of certain people. For example, in Malaysia we used to say stupid like a "COW", in some Arab countries perhaps "DONKEY" became the victim, as "KAZEOL" among the Russian and Central Asian people.

I shoved a 10 Som note (about 3 dollars) into one of the Policemen's palm, grabbed Uda by his sleeve and left the place quickly before, as the Policemen were trying to recollect what had stricken on their head. The swelling crowd witnessing the incident were chattering among themselves. When I glanced back after about 30 meters away, I saw the Policemen were swaying back towards the café. Dr Uda was relieved although there was a trace of fear on his face.

Indeed it was not fun to walk around with Uda at my side. When I walked the street with Uda, the chances that we would be stopped by the Policemen or plain cloth secret service was 90%. During a visit by a foreign dignitary to Kyrgyz Republic, we were stopped at every corner of the street by the Secret Service officials. It was sickening. Other than his dark complexion which was outstanding among the crowd, his long beard had posed a great threat to the security people. The Kyrgyz must have associated his long beard with the Talibans. Back home, Dr Uda had joined a religious group called *Tabligh*[54] and spotting long beard

---

[54] *Tabligh* is a religious movement established in India in 1926

was part of the group's traditions. On several occasions, I suggested that he got rid of that goatee to avoid us from further trouble. However, he was adamant to adhere to the Prophet's tradition.

Tired of all those harassments, I went to see a friend, a Colonel at The Presidential Office. Having stationed at the President's Elite Security Services, he was very influential and highly respected. I came to know him during the official visit of Dr Mahathir two years earlier, when he was assigned to provide the security for the Malaysian Prime Minister. The Colonel gave me his name card with his signature on it, as well as his private mobile number and advised me to show the card to any Tom, Dick and Harry who try to be funny with me. If they became nasty, I just had to wait there and dial his number. I no longer had any trouble after that. I was still being stopped but immediately released, when I shoved the Colonel's name card into their face. I still keep his name card until now. If he is still in the Service, he would have been promoted to the rank of a General.

I was indeed lucky to have two most trusted staff who were loyal to me and they were instrumental in the success of our work in the project. Klichbae had never ceased to give me technical advices so that I could always be on top of the matters, as Aibek looked after overall official and personal matters. He was a smart person in the intellectual sense, although his personal appearance was rather amusing (a young boy with sparkling golden teeth). When he felt that The Policeman who stopped me had taken a longer time than usual to inspect my document, Aibek would ask me in a raised voice;

"Excuse me Sir, do you remember about your appointment with the Deputy Prime Minister next Tuesday?"

---

to undertake voluntary works to spread *dakwah* or revival of Islamic values among Muslim society.

The Policeman who was checking my document suddenly stopped on his track and raised his head to look at Aibek before fixing an intent look at my face.

"Ohhh . . . . thank you for reminding me Aibek . . . . but if I am not mistaken, I had promised General Azimov to take him for a sauna on the same day. Can you ask DPM office to reschedule the meeting . . . ."

With those magic words, the Policeman quickly handed back my document despite his slight irritation, followed by a question if the famous Deputy Police Chief (General Azimov) was my acquaintance. Under certain circumstances, name droppings have been very effective measure to cut red-tapes and bureaucracies.

I left the Kyrgyz Republic in March 2003. However, Aibek was still in contact with me until now and behaves as if I am still his boss, and begged me to take him to Malaysia. He is currently working with an American company in Kandahar, Afghanistan. As Klichbae was computer illiterate, I could only find out about his wellbeing through Aibek when the Latter return to Bishkek for holidays. I hope he still keeps my hunting rifle with him.

Chapter 28

Trekking Along Tien Shan Range

Stretching about 2,500 km from Western Uzbekistan passing through Tajikistan, Kazakhstan, Kyrgyz Republic and connecting to Chinese territory, Tien Shan is one of the longest mountain ranges in the world. Unfortunately, despite its majestic view and unspoiled beauty, not many travellers have explored these territories. Due to rigid travel regulations, as well as lack of infrastructure, tourists and trekkers prefer to visit already the crowded Himalayas or the Andes in South America.

My dream came through, when I was invited to join a group of trekkers to explore the Tien Shan mountain range. I was so excited and spent three months prior to the expedition to keep build up my physical fitness. Tucking my two year-old boy into baby's backpack, I would climb a steep hill behind my house, and ascend towards the distant Alatau Mountain terrains for about two or three hours to strengthen my legs. Otherwise, I would be spending a couple of hours in the gym, carrying out the weight lifting and sit ups.

On the day of the departure, we gathered at one of the prominent hotels in Almaty early in the morning. I was introduced to the other members of the expedition party, a prominent Malaysian businessman Wan Azmi Hamzah (Tan Sri) and his business partner David, a gentleman from Holland, a Vodafone man[55] from London and Dennis Cleary, a former Australian boxer and cyclist. Sergey Guryev from "Alpine XXI" travel agency, who was a veteran trekker would be our guide. He told us that he would be assisted by five local crew members who had already left earlier for the base camp. He said one of them was a female cook who happened to be the only woman in the group. At around 8.00 am we departed to our destination, Kurmyty, a remote village at the foot of Tien Shen, about seven hours drive from Almaty.

Kurmyty, is a remote village located close to Kyrgyz and the Chinese border. From the main road, we had to zigzag our ways for about two hours negotiating winding mountain roads, before we arrived at the destination. It was a settlement of about 200 houses complete with basic facilities such as kindergartens, primary school, police station, clinic, grocery shops, post office, fire brigade, public hall and of course the party headquarters. There was a row of small stalls, which they called *bazaar*, where petty traders were selling some garments, shoes, cosmetics and other house-hold items. Most of the products came from the nearby Chinese neighbour. It was the first sign of market economy, with the emergence of private businesses and entrepreneurship.

---

[55] Vodafone man is a nickname given by the writer when he saw the Holland man used a special Vodafone devices to make calls from remote mountain areas, using nearby satellites.

The settlement was built during the Soviet era in this remote mountain for a specific purpose, and that was to become one of the collective farms for livestock breeding. The territory provides perfect conditions for this purpose, as it has a vast grazing land, excellent climate and clean environment. I was told, during Communist era, Kurmyty used to produce about twenty thousand horses, cattle and pigs and half million sheep annually. Before winter time, most of these livestock would be processed and dispatched to Moscow to feed the Soviet people or perhaps Cuban and Yugoslavian armies as well.

When we arrived, Dinmogamed, our porter, a local horseman and a seasoned trekker was already waiting for us since afternoon. He introduced us to his assistant, a youth in his early twenties. We were late because on our way we stopped to visit Kazakhstan's "grand canyon", and spent a couple of hours admiring this incredible work of nature. The porters quickly loaded our food supplies and other personal items onto eight horses, as the curious onlookers inched closer to examine the visiting foreigners. Children were seen to have paid great interest and expressed admiration at our "imported" camping gears, which were of superior quality and design compared to the Soviet made items, while the elders were interested in foreign visitors, as they incessantly made enquiries to Dinmogamed about us.

At one stage, the porter was visibly annoyed, as he shouted at the meddling crowds, and said how the hell he would know those people, as most of them he had just met for the first time. I understood that the porter didn't mean to be rude, but he was worried because we were running out of time. I came to his rescue by introducing myself and other foreign members of the expedition in their own language to the swelling crowd. Perhaps it was an unwise move, because then they had surrounded me and asked all sorts of questions. One of the middle-aged ladies in the crowd offered to go along with us for the trip. She would carry my backpack and prepare my food, massage my foot, et cetera, followed by witty response from the crowd.

"No! No! Take me! I'm younger and stronger than her!" said another. Then the two ladies started to argue, much to our amusement.

"I was thinking of taking all the ladies in the village with us but then, the men left behind would be lonely without you", I said. Again a chaotic response came from the crowd, however, all were in jovial mood.

When everything was loaded onto the horses, Dinmogamed signalled to one of the elders among the crowd to recite prayers for our safety and wellbeing. I saw the non-Muslims friends in the group also *amin* the prayers. We hurriedly started our journey for the base camp located at the tip of the Tien Shen range. We arrived at the camp when it was already dark. Three large tents were already erected by Sergey's crew who had arrived earlier.

Sergey Guryev gave us a short briefing and offered some ground rules about our expedition that included the do's and don'ts, as well as about safety measures. All members of the expedition party, except me, were seasoned and experienced trekkers. As a last reminder, the Guide told the group including his crew that alcohol was not allowed to be consumed during the expedition. So those who had accidently packed the bottles in their backpacks must empty them that evening. As a result, I witnessed a merry and rowdy bunch of members partying late into the night.

When we woke up the next morning, breakfast was already prepared by the crew. We started our journey soon after breakfast, and I was so excited. There were altogether fourteen of us in the expedition party, six trekkers of foreign nationals, Alexander the guide with his five crew members, Dinmogamed the Porter and his helper, plus nine horses. As agreed with the unwritten rule, all of us should walk and carry our own backpack. Only the porter and his helper would be sitting on horseback. The other horses would carry our foodstuff, cooking utensils and gas balloons.

Donning a camouflage uniform of the Malaysian arm forces, complete with a green beret and combat boot, haversack on my shoulder and in full spirit, I started my first mountain trekking expedition. We began to ascend the high plateau in a straight line. I was among those ahead of the line. The horses, fully loaded with cargo, walked behind the line. It was a steep climb. Despite puffing hard, I felt great and strong, as I continued to surge forward overtaking a few guys in front of me. We followed a narrow track used by previous trekkers. Along the way, we were continuously startled the wild birds, such as quails and pheasants, which flew away noisily as we disturbed their habitat.

After about five hours of scaling the steep slopes, we arrived at a flat land, and the guide instructed us to stop for lunch. I was told that we were standing at about 3,500 meters above the sea level. The guide told us that in a few days we would be walking up the highest plateau of about 4,500 meters above sea level. Nevertheless, I had already felt that I was "on top the world", an achievement registered by my feelings. As I was enthusiastically scaling the steep slope, I didn't have much time to take a good look at the surrounding scene. And here, from this plateau I could see a majestic painting of autumn landscape so beautiful, beyond description.

It was almost the end of September, and the beginning of autumn. The leaves in the forest turned into bright red and yellow covering a vast territory. Meanwhile some species of pines and fir trees grown on the mountain ravines and slopes have maintained their green colour, creating a distinct contrast to the bright red and orange landscape of poplar and birch forest. Meanwhile the large stream with its sparkling water winding its way like a big silver snake, thus displaying a spectacular impact to the great panoramic view.

We continued to enjoy the beautiful scenery as our guide and his helpers were preparing for our lunch. In the meantime, I took the opportunity to get to know the members of our group better. I had met Wan Azmi, who had some business interests in Kazakhstan before this trip. Deep in my heart I kept a great admiration for his business acumen. I also like his business associate, David, a British citizen who made Malaysia his second home. The gentleman from Holland whom I forgot his name was very friendly, well mannered and rather reserved. There was another British guy in the group, who worked for a telecommunications company.

But there was something special about this Aussie whom I thought was charmingly macho. Dennis represented Australian boxing team to Olympic at the time when Mohamed Ali (Cassus Clay) became the Olympic Champion. Then he joined the cycling team and later played rugby. At the age of 63, taller than two meters, Dennis was really fit. We were astonished at his capability to control his breath. While we were puffing and choking like fish out of water, due to the lack of oxygen, as we dragged ourselves up the mountain, Dennis with his explosive thunderous voice that could be heard a kilometre away was talking relentlessly, telling all sort of stories and cracking jokes. Once I said to him;

"You must have a lung as big as that of the horses"

For whatever reason, which was in explicable, I was not comfortable with the Vodafone guy right from the very beginning. So, whenever I encountered this guy, I just greeted him and moved away. Others in the group, including our guide Sergey and his crew, as well as Dinmogamed the porter and his assistant, made up a great company.

The lunch served included sausages and cold cuts of boiled meat and chicken as starters. Wan Azmi and I avoided some of the sausages, as they were made of pork and ham. For the main course we had noodles boiled in horse meat. We had dried fruits, raisins and nuts as dessert. I didn't eat much and grabbed a handful of dried fruit and nuts, and stuffed them in my pocket so that I could chew along the way.

After two hours of rest and lunch break, we continued to ascend the mountain range for another two hours and reached a narrow peak. After a ten-minute break, the Guide told us that we would descend to the other side of mountain. Pointing to a stream down below, Sergey told us that we would spend the night at that place. We had been scaling up the terrain the whole day and then it was time to descend. Apparently, it was more difficult and dangerous to descend than to climb. I slipped a couple of times, and the anxious guide reminded me to be more careful. A fall into the rocky ravine from that altitude could be fatal.

We reached the stream nearly at dusk. Everyone was visibly tired. We unfolded our personal tent and chose the right place to set it up. I set up mine close to that of Wan Azmi's. The crew members set up a large tent which served as our dining hall, as well as their sleeping area.

The temperature fell drastically as the sun set in. We were advised by our guide to clean ourselves at the stream before it would be too cold. I let out a loud cry as soon as I jumped into the stream of ice-cold water.

Our dinner was the leftover from the lunch. It was only the first day and I had already missed home cooked rice and curry. The guide told us that we had covered about 20 kilometres on the first day. He said that next day would be much easier, as we would be trekking along the flat land until we reached the following range. He estimated that we would be able to cover the distance of 40-45 km.

Although I was fit and didn't feel any muscle ache from the first day walk, the most important part of my body, the foot began to take its toll. Perhaps the heavy combat boot or the tender feet pampered for years in the comfort of expensive shoes had caused nasty blisters. The next morning I ditched the combat boot, and put on a pair of snickers borrowed from Wan Azmi. I started early than others, as I knew that the blisters would slow me down. Indeed, I was the last person to arrive at every stop.

On the second day, we were trekking along the stream, formed from melted snow. There were stones at the bottom of the stream and the water was clear. At some part, the stream turned into a raging river and sometimes turned itself into small waterfalls. When the sun appeared from the mountain range, its rays turned the water surface of the stream into reflecting mirrors. Except for the sound of running water from the river, the chirping of birds, songs of insects and husky voice of Jerry, the mountain was calm and provided perfect tranquillity for us to slip into our wildest dreams or fall into deep thought and perhaps revisit our past deeds.

I was thinking, how wonderful it would be if I could have some saving and accumulate enough capital to set up a small factory producing polypropylene woven bags in Almaty. At that time, Kazakhstan didn't have a single PP bag factory and the country was totally dependent on materials imported from China. Since the raw material (PP raisins) was available at Petrochemical complex in the Caspian Sea town of Atyrau, the project could be viable, as such, from a single factory in Almaty, I could expand my business into other towns. Being the first person to venture into this business, there was a great possibility that I would become rich like Wan Azmi.

"Hoi Mike! Why are you smiling alone. If you have a funny story let's share with me?"

Shess! It was Dennis again. Why he had to spoil my dream! The presence of Dennis has brought me back to this earth. I asked Dennis, as we walked side by side about the places he had visited. Apparently, the Aussie had scaled almost all mountain ranges known to people, from his native land of Australia and New Zealand to Himalaya, Alpine, Andes, Kalimanjaro, and some mountains in Chile and Peru. With Dennis, you just need to pop a short question and you would get lengthy answers on any subject. An interesting feature of him was that his seriousness in communicating with you. He told the stories with passion. Perhaps he has never got tired in engaging with people, and therefore he could make it without losing his focus. At the same time, I shared some of the dried fruits I stuffed in my pocket with him.

After a while, I began to fall behind as I could not catch up any longer with Dennis, due to the soaring blisters on my feet. Alone, I get into my inner self and started building my castle in the air. Dreaming is an exciting past time. There were times when it calmed you down. However, there were people who needed external stimulus and extra-venomous agent to move on to this dreaming mode.

In the Malay culture, dreaming is a great past time, and it is no wonder that they have the methos whose central character is *Mat Jenin*[56] who is often preoccupied with daydreaming. One day, while sitting on top of a coconut tree, *Mat Jenin* dreamt that having sold the coconuts, he would board a ship and sail around the world to trade. Upon accumulating sufficient wealth, he would return home and buy a good horse. Mounting the horse he would head for a palace to marry a beautiful princess. At this point, *Mat Jenin* was so absorbed in his dream that he had jolted his "horse" so strongly, whereas he actually pulled the mass of long leaves, typical of coconut palm, snapped, dropping him dead. Although they said that *Mat Jenin* had fallen to his death from the coconut tree, his spirit was still very much alive in many Malay minds. However, the excruciating pain of my feet kept interfering with my *Mat Jenin's* dreams.

I was the last person to arrive at the camp site for the night, literally limping all the way. As expected, when I took off the shoes, the blisters worsen and then blisters started to spread between the fingers of my foot. I began to worry about the following day, and started to discard some personal items from my back pack, in order to reduce the load I would be carrying. After another cold shower and light dinner, I immediately went to sleep because I wanted to take off early the next day. Surprisingly, we had covered about 45 km on the second day.

The morning breeze was fresh with the fragrance of wild flowers and the fallen leaves of birch trees. The crew

---

[56] *Mat Jenin* is one of Malay folktales and it is popular among children.

members were busily preparing for breakfast. I downed a glass of *kefir*[57], and grabbed a few slices of bread and stuffed a handful of dried fruit into my pocket. I met our guide Sergey to enquire about the direction and started off alone, although he insisted that I should have waited for breakfast, as it'll be served soon. The blisters on one of my soles had forced me to walk like an old cowboy who just got down from his long ride, or more like a person who was born with a pair of "bow-legs". Slowly, I headed towards the mountain as pointed by Sergey, walking among the poplar and birch trees, which began to shed orange coloured leaves along the river bank.

Again, I was drowning in my deep thought. I started to ponder what I would be like when I reached forty and my accomplishment in life. I started to reflect upon myself whether I had fulfilled my duty satisfactorily, and whether I had succeeded in building my staff and the organization that I worked with. Not with standing, had I been fair to my family? Above all, as a grateful son, have I fulfilled the expectations of my parents? So were my siblings, had I forgotten the good old days when we were raised?

At that point in time, I wasn't sure if I were a good man, a loving husband, a caring father and a worthy son who had not abandoned his parents. And most importantly, have I fulfilled all my obligations to my Creator for bestowing me the most decent livelihood. All this while, I have neglected my eternal need to be constantly thankful to my Creator, the Almighty. Or perhaps the right case was the fact that I missed the opportunity to look back.

I didn't realise how long I had been walking, half conscious, as my critical mind was analysing all those

---

[57]   *Kefir* is a fermented milk or sour milk in Russian language.

questions, when suddenly I found myself standing at the foot of a tall mountain. As I looked back, I saw Dennis's tall figure in the distance ahead of the group heading towards my direction. Throwing down the backpack on the ground, I emptied my bladder and took a short rest before the big climb.

It took us three hours of painstaking effort to reach the peak of the mountain. At some places, the climb was so steep and dangerous, as a slip from the guy ahead of us would cause "stone showers" on the persons below. When a golf player hit the ball wild, he would shout "ball!!!" to alert others. Here we screamed "stone shower!!!" As we ascended higher, we had breathing difficulty due to lack of oxygen. I paused at every ten steps to regularise and recover my breathing. It was a real physical as well as mental challenge. At the beginning, I wasn't sure if I could reach the peak due to the awful condition of my feet. Nevertheless, I still could complete my hiking day after day.

While our expedition has entered the seventh day, the condition of my feet has worsened. The blistered skins came off leaving red flesh exposed at the sole of both my feet, and parts between the fingers. Those around me just shook their heads in disbelief at my agony. Some suggested that I should continue on horseback, as the unwritten rule no longer applies under such circumstances. But I said I would continue on foot as long as I could. When the gentleman from Holland examined my foot, he said he could do something about it. He then took out an emergency aid box from his rucksack, and started to clean my wound with the spirit as I was screaming in pain. He then pasted a material like a plaster but much thicker and softer, which he said was a newly invented artificial skin at my foot sole, and told me not to remove it until I came home. The artificial skin proved to be very effective, as it removed a lot of my sufferings till the very end of our expedition.

David was praising my courage for keeping on walking under such a condition. He narrated an incident about a woman who suffered similar chronic blisters like mine during one of his expeditions to the Himalayas. The poor woman was pleading to be left alone to die in the mountain, as she could no longer take another step. Finally, they had to carry her on a stretcher until the end of the expedition. Dennis quipped, saying that in my case they would not be carrying me on a stretcher as it was easier to "put me to sleep" instead.

Then, I became lively and back to high spirit, after I got the "artificial skin" and proposed to Dinmogamed that we went for rabbit hunting in the evening. He agreed, and we set out on horseback. As the other horses were tired after the whole day's walk with the heavy load, we decided to take the horse he was mounting, and both of us sat on the lone horse. Apparently, we need to cross to the other side of the bank. I enquired if the horse could take two of us at the same time through the raging river. Dinmogamed told me to relax, and assured me that his mount could safely take us across. Indeed, without hesitation, Dinmogamed's horse with two men on its back waded into the raging river, stepping cautiously on slippery stones of ice-cold water. We had to raise our feet and sit cross-legged in order not to get wet, at some part of the river as the water reached close to the shoulder of our mount. I was praying hard, while Dinmogamed just chuckled at my anxiety. The Kazakh mountain horses were so strong and special, that I would devote a paragraph about them later.

When we reached the other side of the river bank, Dinmogamed jumped off the horse and handed a rifle to me. He gave the honour to me as his guest to do the killing. There were hundreds of fat rabbits running around the mountain foot. I galloped the horse like a cowboy in the Wild West, and fired from the horseback, but missed most of them. Dinmogamed shouted in the distance, and told me that it was not the way to shoot the rabbits.

"Let them run and you don't chase. In a short distance, they would stop, only then you fire!"

I did as he said but soon lost the thrill. Somehow I felt bad, like shooting someone in the back during a duel; a very ungentlemanly act. It was different when the animal was running, as if he was mocking at me and challenging me . . . . Hey dude . . . . come and get me if you can . . . . You moron! You can't even shoot straight!.

We collected the fallen animal, and rode back to the camp site. That evening we had *grilled wild rabbit* on our menu.

As promised, I would like to share some information about the Kazakh mountain horses. This special breed of horses lived in the mountainous region of Kazakhstan and Kyrgyz Republic. They are medium sized built and for a fully grown weighing from 400-450 kg. Their bodies are compact with strong and big leg bones. The horses grown thick hair during winter. Found mostly in dark brown or black. Having withstood cold winter in their natural habitat, the horses have adapted well to severe conditions, and possessed special quality not to be found in other breeds.

These horses can scale vertical slopes, and balanced themselves on narrow path of the mountain ravines. They are brave and clever. In some places, we had to tread carefully on a very narrow path at high attitude. A small slip would cause one's life, as we were exposed to a free fall into the rocky ravines 500 meters below. Even for us, the daredevil human beings were sometimes scared. And the ordinary horses would not dare to venture a step into such situation, but those mountain horses with at least 200 kilos of loads on their backs would never hesitate to pull through the tough mission. It was fascinating to watch how these horses balanced themselves. If the ravine was on the left, they would lean their body to the right, so that if they slipped, they would not be rolling down the mountain. Sometimes, stones under their front legs would give way during scaling. Under such circumstances, these animals would bend their front knees until they touched the ground, so that the heavy weight on their back would not drag them down. Nevertheless, Dinmogamed told me that there were few incidents, when those horses fell to their death on those mountain paths.

Dinmogamed narrated to me about one of British trekkers, a woman who suffered a broken leg during the expedition. He sat that woman on one of his horses which safely took her out of the mountain right to a clinic in Cholpon-Ata, a lake town in the Kyrgyz Republic. After the woman was discharged from a hospital, she pleaded Dinmogamed to sell her the horse that saved her life at any price, for she wanted to take the animal back with her to England. Dinmogamed enquired which part of England she lived. She told him Manchester. Shaking his head Dinmogamed said he would offer the horse for free if Manchester happened to have a mountain nearby. The horse would not survive the flat land.

After the rabbit hunting, Dinmogamed became close with me. Furthermore, we could communicate freely, as I speak fluent Russian. Sometimes he would ask me to walk with him at the back of the line. When we fall back far behind, he would offer me his horse as he shared a mount with his assistant. At first I didn't agree, as I felt it was like cheating. But then, having considered myself an "invalid" I could not resist the temptation. By now, the readers already knew about my obsession for horses. I jumped into the saddle and galloped the horse while letting out huge cry like the Red Indians in the movies.

From a distance, I saw a figure of a lone colleague at the back of the line. I decided to tease him. Galloping the horse at a breakneck speed, while screaming like a crazy Indian, I rushed towards the lone trekker who didn't notice my presence, until it was too late and too close. I guessed the Vodafone man was so absorbed in his fantasy when he realized that he was "attacked" by the mountain man. The Vodafone man shrieked and fell to the ground in terror. I could see his face which look like a dead person, and regretted my act. After regained his composure, he yelled at me;

"You Moron! Why you have to do that!".

Under normal circumstances, I would have smacked his face for such words. However, it was clearly my fault, so I profusely apologized to the angry man, and admitted that I behaved foolishly.

I only narrated about the incident to Wan Azmi, who just smiled and said that luckily the guy didn't have a heart attack. From that moment, I tried to avoid the Vodafone man. He also looked at me full of hatred in his eyes. There was a peculiar behaviour of the Vodafone man. He used to take shower naked, and allowed everyone to see his dangling libido. Wan Azmi remarked that he fit to be an actor in a pornographic movie. "Provided he could last long . . .", I added as we laughed at his antic.

Somehow, fate has changed my hostile relationship with the Vodafone man. One day, he requested to sit on horseback when crossing the stream, as he didn't want to wet his shoes. Dinmogamed instructed his assistant to take the man across the stream. The boy sat the man on the saddle, and led the horse to the other side of the stream. However, after reaching the other side, the boy carelessly let go of the rein, and went to pick up something nearby. As the Vodafone man was dismounting, the horse suddenly walked away, and the rider's left leg was caught in the stirrups.

The Vodafone man fell on his back, hanging upside down as his left leg was still caught in the stirrups. The horse continued to drag the man over rugged stone, as he was screaming in pain. The careless boy was startled and froze in his trail. Although the Vodafone man and I were not comfortable to each other, I rushed to grab the reins and relieved the man's leg from the stirrups. He thanked me and hurled abusive curses at the boy. At one point, the truly irritated Vodafone man rushed to punch the young boy, but I quickly restrained him. He continued cursing the boy until dinner time, and ordered Dinmogamed to chase the boy back to where he belonged. During the dinner he thanked me again, and said if not for my quick action, he would have been dead or suffered broken head. I overheard Dinmogamed was reminding the boy that if he wanted to stay alive, he should stay far away from the Vodafone man.

During one of the nights, I felt the weather was extremely cold. I gathered some dead branches that I could find near the river bank, and started a bonfire. Soon, the crew helped me to collect more logs and branches and we sat near the fire to warm ourselves before we went to bed. I woke up around six in the morning, as I felt a strong urge to empty my bladder. I was baffled as I stepped out of the tent. The whole place was covered with snow, and all my colleagues have disappeared. How could they leave without me? Perhaps they were not aware that I was left behind, but then why they had to leave before dawn? I waded through knee deep snowfall, while being absorbed in my thought, and tried to figure out why I was left alone until, suddenly my foot got caught in a rope and I tumbled on something. I heard a loud scream from under the heap of snow.

"What the hell is it!"

By then, I already knew that I had tumbled on Dennis's tent which was fully covered with snow. I dug the startled man out from the snow piles. We were astonished in disbelieve that the whole mountain was turned into white field, even our tents were also "disappeared" under thick snow blanket. Our commotion has woken up few other colleagues. Tien Shan already has snow fall in early October! However, a few sunny days in a row after that have turned back the mountain once again into a colourful landscape.

I had lost at least five kg after the ten-day walk. I lost my appetite. At the beginning of the trip, David was telling me that during his expedition to the Himalaya, they were only served with *chappati* (flat bread made of wheat flour) eaten with *dal* curry (split peas cooked in curry flavour). They had the same food everyday during the whole expedition. After a few days, they only discharged a "chicken poop" when they went to toilet. I thought he was joking, but soon I discovered that he was telling the truth. Since I had burned a lot of calories during the whole day walk, while eating less, I was shivering at night, forcing me to wake up a few times to warm myself at the bonfire.

Sometimes Wan Azmi would ask me to share his tent, as it was rather large to accommodate two of us. I loved to hear all sorts of stories "from the horse's mouth". We talked about many issues ranging from business to politics. One day late into the night, he was telling me about a big sum of money he was trusted to keep by a certain man named Daim, when a certain political party was declared illegal by the Malaysian court. What was he talking about? Who was this Daim and what political party that was disbanded by the court . . . . ? I simply couldn't understand Malaysian politics, and I think it was too complicated. It's better for me to stay away as far as possible.

We have seen so many beautiful sites along the journey. The beauty of Tien Shan was beyond description. For me, it was the first mountain trekking, and therefore my words didn't carry weight. But those seasoned trekkers like Wan Azmi, David and Dennis who have scaled numerous mountains all over the world have also testified about the unspoiled beauty of Tien Shan. When we stopped for a rest at some of the most beautiful sites, I would be the last person to leave. I would tell others;

"You all move on because I have decided to build a home and settle down at this place".

During an official visit to Kyrgyz Republic in 1999, Tun Dr Mahathir was taken on a helicopter ride by Ashkar Akaev, the ousted Kyrgyz President, overflying some parts of Tien Shan. I was told that the Malaysian Prime Minister was so amazed that he was jokingly requested for a small plot of land to enable him to build a house at this place after his retirement.

I read somewhere that God the Almighty has created paradise so beautiful beyond the imagination of any human being. Well, I have no complaint if I would be given a place just like this in the next life, even if it happens to be the lowest ranking of God's paradise.

On the fourteenth day of our trip, we hit the rock. As a matter of fact, we had arrived at a glacier and if I was not mistaken, it was part of the famous Inylchek glacier which stretched for 60km from the Central Tien Shan Range. The slippery frozen surface of ice layers made it impossible for the horses to scale. Even the trekkers had to change their snickers into wearing spiked shoes.

A decision was made that Dinmogamed should return back to Kurmyty with most of the travelling equipment. They also decided that I should accompany the Porters to ensure the safety of those personal belongings. I was told that by hook or by crook, I must arrive in Kurmyty in two days time, and I must head straight to Almaty with all those gears because Wan Azmi, David and Jerry would proceed to Nepal for another expedition. While I was figuring out how it could be possible to make a fourteen day's journey into a two-day trip even on horseback, they shouted at me to move fast instead of wasting more time.

"Prove to us that you are a real Jigit", they threw a challenge. At the same time I was happy that the gruelling expedition ended there, not knowing what was waiting for me next.

Dinmogamed unloaded the cargo from one of the horses, and loaded onto other horses, saddled it and handed the animal as my mount. We started our journey immediately on a trot. Horse riding was fun if it is a joy ride. Taking a horse for a leisure walk could be a pleasant experience. It would be a thrill when you gallop the horse. However, your whole body would shake when you are trotting for a long period. In our case we could not afford to walk at leisure, as we were running out of time. At the same time, we could not make the horses galloped, because they were carrying heavy cargoes. So we trotted the whole day, until our clattering bones felt like dropping off and our butt felt numbed.

At some places, the climb was so steep and dangerous. We rode the whole day, and only stopped for ten minutes to have a quick lunch. Dinmogamed took a different route home. We walked on a vast plateau, where a single tree could not be found. What I saw was a stretch of endless large grass field. There was no sign of lives on the vast plain. However, Dinmogamed told me that there were packs of wolves roaming around at night. I was alarmed. We continued with our journey until dusk. Dinmogamed said he wanted to cover another ten kilometres before we stopped for the night. However, one of the horses was so exhausted that she refused to walk, despite all the pulling and whippings. We had to call it a day. I was so tired and hungry.

Dinmogamed's assistant set up a single tent for three of us to share, as Dinmogamed was relieving the burden from horses. They were let loose to graze around our tent. I had left with only two small cans of tuna and a loaf of bread for our dinner. We swallowed a meagre meal in less than three minutes, and washed down with the last bottle of plain water. I requested Dinmogamed to remove the blanket from the tent, as I couldn't stand the stinking smell of horses' sweat on the blanket. They laughed at my antic. We took turn on a watch duty. Dinmogamed said he didn't want to take a chance as the howling of wolves getting nearer and nearer to our camp. Perhaps the hungry pack has detected our smell. When the howling got too close, the horses became restless. Dinmogamed fired his rifle into the air to deter the wild animals from attacking our scared horses.

We continued our journey at dawn without breakfast, and trotted for hours. Exhausted, hungry and thirsty, pain all over the body, all I had. I kept asking Dinmogamed hundreds of time when we will be arriving at Kurmyrty. I just wanted to be home, hugged my woman and asked her to cook some *rendang* [58] and boil some spicy soup. The Kazakh kept telling me "not far away", "soon", "a short distance". It was an endless journey to me. I wondered how Genghis Khan (The Kazakh called Chengiz Khan) and his army could travel thousands of mile non-stops during their campaign in these regions. So did Alexander the Great and his Macedonian warriors.

Meanwhile, I have discovered a more comforting way to ride. Since we were travelling on a vast plain, I could see Dinmogamed a kilometre away. So I let him trotted his way, while I walked my horse until I saw a small figure of him in the distance. Then I would gallop my horse. As soon as I caught up with him, I halted the horse, and directed her into a walking mode again. Alternately I would gallop and walk most of the remaining journey. By engaging in this trick, I no longer suffered the bone-shaking consequences of the trotting horse.

Dinmogamed once narrated to me that when he was a young boy, he ventured into the vast plain and lost his way home, as he wandered around till nightfall. Then it began to snow. He crawled under the belly of his horse and lighted a small fire from woollen material taken from under the saddle. The Kazakh used to put a piece of cloth on the horseback before they saddled the horse. As he was praying hard and imagined horrific death from cold or vicious attack of a pack of hungry wolves, he heard the footstep or rather hoof stamp approaching in the dark. Apparently, a *chobon* (shepherd) from the distant village was looking for his

---

[58] *Rendang* is a spicy meat dish and it is traditionally prepared by the Malays community during festive occasions such as *Hari Raya Aidilfitri* and *Hari Raya Aidilhadha*.

missing horse had seen the light, and came to the rescue of the young fellow.

Dinmogamed's story prompted me to ask if he was sure that we were on the right track. The two Kazakhs busted into laughter. We descended into the lower terrain and came to a small stream. I jumped from the saddle and rushed to satisfy my thirst. The horses also drank from the stream. Dinmogamed told me that within two hours, we would be arriving at the settlement of the last shepherd living in that area, who happened to be his distant relative. I simply hope that this time he would be telling the truth. Indeed, after about two hours ride, I could see from the distance, a hut perched at the mountain slope, and a figure of a man working near a pile of hay.

The man threw his shovel, when he saw us approaching and a woman appeared from somewhere to greet us. They ushered us into their small hut. As a matter of fact it was a *yurta* (Kazakh round-shaped mobile home used from ancient time by the nomadic tribes). Incidentally, for the first time in my life, I lost my manners. Before our hosts could open their mouth to invite us to eat, I grabbed a loaf of "non" (flat bread), spread some homemade butter clumsily on it and stuffed them in my mouth. With my mouth full of food, I profusely apologized, telling that I was so hungry after two days of non-stop riding without food. Our hosts took a pitiful look at me, and shoved a cup into my hand, tea mixed with fresh milk. He must have anticipated that I could probably choke from the food. Alone, I finished two pieces of flat bread and numerous cup of milk tea. It was only plain "non", homemade butter and tea, but it was one of the most delicious meals I have ever enjoyed. Our hosts wanted to slaughter a lamb but we told them we could not afford to waste anymore time.

As we hurriedly prepared to take leave, I shoved a hundred dollar note into the wife's hand, left my number, and invited them to visit me if they happened to be in Almaty. Visibly embarrassed, they refused to take my small gift, until Dinmogamed convinced them that it was a great honour for me if they took the money. I could not imagine about the couple who spent most of their entire lives in those remote mountains, far from other people and civilization to earn a living raising livestock. Sex was probably the best entertainment they could afford. I guessed this particular couple would stay married, till death took them apart.

We arrived in Kurmyty in the afternoon. Someone was already waiting to take me to Almaty. We had a shower and tea at Dinmogamed's house. Dinmogamed was flat on his back on *kurpacha* (soft mattress a familiar item in most of Central Asian homes), and parted with me with the same position as I took leave. He was too exhausted, and suffered back ache. Shaking his head, he conferred me the status of the best "Jigit", for I still could run around, and now would be heading to Almaty. We have covered about 450 km of Tien Shan range in two days.

I hope one day I could afford to own a horse brought in from Kazakhstan, and take part in the Malaysian endurance race. At the moment, I am still a *Jigit Without His Horse.*